Cryptocurrency & Altcoin Investing For Beginners 2022

Web 3.0 & Smart Contracts
Blockchain Technology

Contents

Analytical Tools and Project Websites

Using Social Media as News Source

Having a Network will help a lot.

Doing Your Homework

CONCLUSION

INTRODUCTION

Since the beginning of the human race, people have sought out many freedoms, including financial freedom; the free will to spend their hard-earned money, and their choice of making their investments. Traditional finance controlled by bank institutions and governments through its many organs of finance did not offer financial freedom in totality.

The cryptocurrency was invented in 2009, and Bitcoin a decentralized form of finance without a central unit of government. Since then, many cryptocurrencies have been formed, and they offer all manner of financial freedoms in the modern era of technology. The current global news on crypto and the unavoidable trends on cryptocurrency are why you are reading this book, and you will not get disappointed.

A guide is required for everything that makes up our daily lives; a manual to execute a task, do it to perfection, and finance is no different. In this book, I have detailed for you step by step how to thrive as a beginner investor in the crypto market. This book will find all the information you require to understand the new financial era and innovation.

The cryptocurrency market has been met with criticism and support in almost an equal measure. The top-tier business moguls in the global economy fall on any side of the coin, with Elon Musk and Bill Gates in support and Warren Buffet, who doesn`t support the market. All said and done, and millionaires have been born out of cryptocurrency, who knows you could be the next? Let me help you do that.

Cryptocurrency success stories

Bitcoin and Altcoin millionaires are the new normal for traders and investors. From Mid 2018 the crypto market boomed, and the financial sector is gaining more tycoons. This amazes me because crypto is yet to reach its full potential. Affluent cryptocurrencies such as bitcoin, ethereum, Litecoin, and ripple have succeeded where others haven't. Some success stories include:

- Roger Ver is a crypto phenomenon and one of the earliest bitcoin investors and is known to advocate for bitcoin, and his crypto wealth stands at $520 million.

- Mr. Smith is a mysterious investor who chose to stay out of the social media frenzy and was interviewed by Forbes magazine in incognito mode. As a software engineer, he understood the market better and made a fortune out of it.

- Eric Finman started investment in crypto as a teenager. Within a year, he sold out his investments and started his own company that gives crypto tutorials in video form. He also pays his employees in cryptocurrencies.

- Jeremy Gardener owns a crypto castle in San Francisco where cryptocurrency entrepreneurs reside. He was a self-made millionaire at the age of 25. He started the crypto journey by buying crypto from his friends in exchange for fiat currencies.

The Crypto Ecosystem

Decentralized Finance (DeFi) has been a light in a dark crypto market, with it came a way to survive the daily market world. Digital currencies have been translated from online platforms to the physical world; goods and services can now be purchased and paid for in cryptocurrencies.

With a hot market like this, new investors decide to start trade without proper research, which does not end well. In this book, we (you and I) should fully understand the following concepts: the DeFi blueprint, lending platforms, Smart Contracts, blockchain technology, how decentralized finance operates, and the revolution the financial world has received.

Traditional finance is a market that requires proper education. There are university degrees that cater to financial literacy and business investments, mainly making money and staying wealthy. Students have been taught how to survive economic tough times and still win. Cryptocurrency, however, has not received much educational light, and that is why I am here.

Understand this; the crypto market will make or break your wealth. Without proper research and personal understanding of the market, you can best be assured you will lose. On the other hand, the more prepared and well equipped you are, the higher your chances of survival in the crypto era.

How does trade work? Simply put, you need to have the capital, make a purchase or make an investment, make profits, and use your hard-earned money to make purchases that make life better and easier for you; you can also give back to society in charity. Cryptocurrency started in 2009 with bitcoin, and Altcoins (Alternative for bitcoin) have graced the market in recent years. This book will cover Cryptocurrency trade.

I will walk you through everything that makes the past, present, and future of cryptocurrency. How it started, why it started, the progress that has been achieved ever since, the ups and downs the market has incurred, and the future projects that have been proposed to work for the better of DeFi.

After you have weighed all your options presented to you by the global market concerning Bitcoin and Altcoins, and you have decided to invest in the cryptocurrency market, then you are at the right place. I have written this book specifically for you. This is just not literature and a theoretical review of how I think you should make your investments.

Every bit of available information here is something I have personally tried and proved. Not just me, but other incredible and notable crypto investors I have the privilege to know and trade with. So, buckle up and enjoy the read: before we get started, it is worth noting that the cryptocurrency market works in your favor.

Section 1: Starting With the Fundamentals

Chapter 1: Stepping Out From the Conventional

When looking to raise capital to set up or expand your business, the first place to start is usually the bank. For many small businesses, raising funds through financial institutions is a time-tested means. Simply put, traditional finance means a line of credit secured through conventional methods, primarily based under the '4 Cs': character, collateral, capital, and capacity.

The traditional financing approach is relatively standardized. The financier will evaluate your credit history, business plan, and your assets to determine your qualifications. The most widely used traditional financing source is through conventional loans from large and small financial institutions with the application procedure highly reliant on rigid, statistical factors such as your credit score. Smaller banks are more likely to award a loan than big banks, which have rigorous requirements.

Apart from banks, small businesses can obtain financing through credit unions who are much more favorable. Unlike banks, credit unions are nonprofit organizations that the members own. Credit unions have limitations on who can join, restricting participation to the residents of a particular community or the affiliates of a specific institution.

Credit unions can at times offer loans at more favorable interest rates than banks due to their nonprofit affiliation. However, for both banks and credit unions, conventional lines of credit have high interest rates compared to modern financing means such as fintech solutions and blockchain-based decentralized finance or DeFi. We will look at what decentralized finance is later in this book. For now, let's find out the flaws of the legacy financial system.

What Is Wrong With It?

The financial meltdown of 2008 triggered the beginning of constant reforms in the entire banking terrain. The future of finance is rapidly changing, and legacy banks streamline their institutional framework to minimize overhead expenses and prioritize their fundamental aptitudes instead of trying to succeed in every aspect.

Following the advent of financial technology, popularly known as fintech, startups, industries, and internet banking companies looking to take advantage of the vulnerabilities of big banks proves that the banking system must be on par with the changing times. Below are the critical problems facing the legacy financial architecture in today's world of cryptocurrencies and decentralized finance:

• Low-interest rates: Physical banks are known for their low or no interest rates at all on savings accounts. In February 2020, the median annual percentage yield(APY)for savings accounts in the United States was 0.09 percent. The key reason why savings accounts yield low-interest rates is that banks make substantial gains when the rates of the funds they lend out as loans are much higher than the rate they pay people who deposit funds into savings accounts.

Another reason why banks offer negligible interest rates is because they have won a substantial portion of the market share. There is no contentious rivalry with other banks for business, according to a study by Itamar Drechsler, a professor of finance at the University of Pennsylvania.

• Slow digital transformation: the legacy financial model has been overwhelmingly slow in undertaking digital regeneration. Their online impression has been hugely limited to primary functions such as deposits, withdrawals, transfers, loan applications, and settling bills. As such, traditional financial institutions have been unable to enjoy the advantages of full-scale state-of-the-art IT solutions.

A study conducted by the Massachusetts Institute of Technology (MIT) notes that digital transformation can minimize the cost of banking by a whooping 60-80 percent. Nevertheless, a sluggish transition to the digital realm has ensured banks cannot compete feasibly in the contemporary landscape.

- Barriers of legacy architecture: the legacy infrastructure of core banking solutions (CBS) and standard data packages are still being utilized by many banks worldwide. Back in the days, this contemporary infrastructure could offer a dash of steadiness and safety. However, with the advancement in technology and the introduction of quicker and more flexible alternatives, the scope of these threadbare systems has slowly started being eaten away.

- Stringent regulatory framework: Every legacy bank must comply with the regulatory standards set by its oversight bodies. For example, the RBI in India requires commercial banks to maintain a capital-asset ratio, a cash reserve ratio, and a statutory liquidity ratio.

Likewise, US and western banks must comply with PSD-2 and MiFID requirements. Failure to comply would see these banks slapped with a considerable misconduct penalty. In actuality, it is estimated that global banks are paying nearly $270 million annually to comply with the authorities.

- Inappropriate client assistance: One of the significant impacts of the 2008 financial crisis was that many customers lost confidence in the current financial system. For this reason, most financial institutions introduced a wide variety of services to try and restore the lost trust.

When product comparison, access to information, and making resentments have become extremely easy, financial institutions need to avoid messing around and falling short. Client needs should be addressed with the significance they deserve. However, the banks are yet to satisfy their clients' needs, and most people have opted for alternative solutions such as 'Cryptocurrencies'.

How is Cryptocurrency Different?

Blockchain technology and cryptocurrencies are arguably the most significant innovations in the financial industry, at least following the events of 2008. During the peak of the recession, many people lost their asset value resulting in a loss of confidence in the centralized financial system. People lost money, homes, assets, and belongings to the government. The traditional financial system has reached a state where governments are using the law to steal people's property.

It is time for people to store their asset value in a platform where the government cannot get close. The advent of Bitcoin by the anonymous Satoshi Nakamoto using blockchain technology came as a savior from the troubles of the traditional financial system. Most people who have no idea what Bitcoin is were skeptical of the technology. However, as people began generating wealth using the crypto assets, more and more people started believing in the new system. The acceptance of Bitcoin has become more widespread nowadays, with the pioneering cryptocurrency reaching a total market capitalization of $1 trillion in 2021.

The main attraction towards Bitcoin and cryptocurrencies is decentralization. In addition to other benefits such as speed and transparency, cryptocurrencies are highly secure. The blockchain technology that powers cryptocurrency assets is solid so that hackers cannot get past it. As such, many people worldwide have started feeling more comfortable around the blockchain ecosystem and using cryptocurrencies like Bitcoin.

Today, more than 10,000 cryptocurrencies circulate in the market, with Bitcoin ranked as the world's most prominent due to its mammoth market capitalization. Cryptocurrencies act as an alternative to the conventional financial system and curtail most of the risks and challenges associated with it. Having used a bank myself, I'm aware of how complicated and slow they are: a ton of paperwork, high charges, and the time taken to move a vast amount of funds.

Cryptocurrencies vs. Traditional Financial System

Decentralized vs. centralized

The government controls the traditional financial system. Bitcoin and altcoins are powered by distributed ledger technology, decentralized, and out of control from any monetary authority or government body. When transacting using cryptocurrencies, there is no need for involving intermediaries such as banks.

In the blockchain ecosystem, the network is distributed among the users, and every member is responsible for validating transactions, unlike banks which control all the transactions made by their users. In the cryptocurrency ecosystem, everyone is equal, and nobody can overrule the other users.

Security

The centralized conventional financial system requires third parties to intermediaries to manage your finances and information. If the system is undermined, the security of your finances and financial information is at risk too. Blockchain and digital assets made sure that we can transact both domestically and internationally in a secure way. Cryptocurrencies are transacted in a peer-to-peer system that does not require the involvement of third parties.

Access and anonymity

The credit/debit cards provided by financial institutions contain the personal information of their owners. As such, the information can be used to monitor the spending activity of the owners, and when in the wrong hands, the information can be used to steal funds or impersonification. On the contrary, cryptocurrency transactions are entirely anonymous, and there are no personal details involved. Digital assets are transacted through a random string of alphanumeric addresses, making it hard to track down the owner.

Additionally, digital currencies are easily accessible since they exist on the blockchain, accessed through the internet. You don't have to travel to a brick-and-mortar building located some distance away from you to access your funds. All you need is a smartphone device or a computer and internet connection to spend your money.

Speed and transaction cost

Eliminating third parties in transaction processes also cuts down the involved cost and the processing time. Banks involve many manual paperwork and procedures, which involves a lot of costs and time-consuming procedures. Moving vast sums of money globally using traditional systems can take days or even weeks before the transaction is completed. On the other hand, cryptocurrency transactions are almost instant, and the transaction cost is massively reduced.

The Future That Is Crypto

Decentralization through cryptocurrencies is the right direction in the evolution of finance, banking, and investment. Digital currencies are filling up the gaps left by the conventional banking and financial system blank. However, many people worldwide are still skeptical to accept them due to the lack of understanding of how they function.

Cryptocurrencies, like fiat currency, lets you purchase goods and services or even trade them to generate profit. These cryptos are underpinned by a robust digital ledger protected by solid cryptographic technology and accessed through an internet connection.

Although cryptocurrencies have existed for only a little over a decade, they have developed into a global phenomenon. Many people have been attracted to this industry due to the luxuries involved with investing in these digital assets. They are characterized by massive prize volatility, and traders and investors alike take advantage of these price swings to generate profits. Many people believe Bitcoin and cryptocurrencies are the future of payments, finance, and investment.

In 2019, the German Deutsche bank stated that the current fiat system appears fragile and might be replaced by crypto before 2030. According to the bank, the high inflation and "decades of low labor costs" could push people towards alternative currencies such as crypto and gold, driving their value. Deutsche Bank's report further notes that the number of cryptocurrency users will multiply by four by 2030, reaching 200 million active users.

There are several reasons why cryptocurrencies have become popular among their users. First of all, cryptocurrencies are perceived as the future by many people who believe their full potential is yet to be realized. Many people are now racing towards acquiring them before they hit their peak value in the future.

Other people prefer cryptocurrencies since they eliminate the need for banks and central authorities to manage money issuance. This makes cryptocurrencies inflation-proof compared to fiat currencies whose supply is controlled by central banks and governments.

Moreover, other supporters of Bitcoin are fans of the technology behind it. The distributed ledger technology is a decentralized, immutable recording platform that guarantees safety and transparency. Others are speculators who capitalize on short-term price movements to generate profits.

All in all, cryptocurrencies have significant advantages, and their massive surge in value shows how their demand has grown over the years. The crypto industry is at a tipping point, like any other technology, where it reaches a point of no return. Institutions and big banks have already begun investing in cryptocurrencies endorsing their adoption even further.

There's More Than One System

As of May 2021, there are over 10,000 different existing digital currencies, according to Blackspot. That is way more than the total number of fiat currencies across the globe. Many people ask the question: why are there so many of them circulating in the market? Just over ten years ago, only Bitcoin existed, and it paved the way for an influx of many different coins, all serving various purposes. Today, there is a cryptocurrency in virtually every sector of the economy.

Cryptocurrencies leverage the underlying blockchain technology to revolutionize various sectors such as finance, health, entertainment, data storage, energy, social network, supply and logistics, and the arts and content creation industry. Blockchain technology provides developers with an opportunity to create different digital currencies to perform different functions. This is one of the key reasons why there are very many cryptocurrencies in the market today.

There are those cryptocurrencies that function as a means of payment for goods and services. These cryptocurrencies also tend to act as a store of value and can very much assume the roles of traditional fiat currencies. Bitcoin, Litecoin, Bitcoin Cash, Digibyte, and pretty much very many others fall under this category. Bitcoin is the most popular not only in this category but in the entire cryptocurrency industry.

On the other hand, there are those that power flexible building blockchains as opposed to payment means. Blockchain platforms powered by these types of cryptocurrencies allow develo[pers to build other services and cryptocurrencies on top of them. Ethereum, TRON, EOS, and Ripple are a few examples of cryptocurrencies that fall under this category. Ethereum network is the most popular under this category, especially for the creation of decentralized finance (DeFi) platforms.

DeFi is an umbrella term used to describe various applications and services in the public blockchain space, which is focused on disrupting the conventional financial system using smart contracts. Smart contracts are enforceable agreements that are executed autonomously and accessed by anybody with an internet connection.

DeFi's P2P protocols and applications are built on decentralized blockchains. They require no intermediaries or permission, allowing easy access to financial services such as lending, borrowing, and even trading financial instruments through decentralized exchanges. Today, most DeFi applications are hosted by the Ethereum network, although other upcoming rivals are more superior, quicker, cheaper, and more scalable.

Decentralized finance has enabled the introduction of plenty of opportunities that bring about an open, trustless, and robust financial system. The ecosystem is still in its infancy, with a total value (TVL) of $43 billion in various assets currently locked under DeFi products. We will learn more about this developing ecosystem in the following chapters.

Chapter 2: Focusing On Decentralized Finance

What is Decentralized Finance?

Decentralized finance is, in short, financial freedom, freedom from traditional financial institutions, and control from the governments. Decentralized finance (DeFi) is an independent financial ecosystem that allows users to control their financial assets and how they use those assets without the involvement of banks or governments.

Towards the end of 2019 to date, DeFi has seen rapid growth as more assets have been locked in the ecosystem. DeFi uses blockchain technology, whose basic idea is to store data so that it cannot be changed, manipulated, or controlled by any central actor. The uses of this technology may revolutionize the future of the global economy.

The need for DeFi comes from the need to make financial services available to everyone worldwide. More than 1.7 billion people worldwide have no access and means to adequate financial services, which solves the current existing problem from traditional financial infrastructures. Examples of pure DeFi include Uniswap, MarkerDAO, and Compound, which serve as digital asset exchange, decentralized autonomous organization, and a lending protocol.

Most of these DeFi platforms use decentralized apps known as Dapps. They use smart contracts to execute financial transactions making them faster, extra sufficient, and more affordable to use than traditional financial systems. Dapps are not subjected to the case of bias because computer codes govern them.

DeFi projects aim to make investing and trading more accessible and affordable, as long as one has a smartphone gadget, internet connection, and a trading platform. DeFi offers outstanding loans known as `Flash Loans` taken and paid back within a single transaction and allows traders to maximize profits across different platforms.

Hybrid versions of DeFi have emerged, intending to blend DeFi and traditional banking; they are called CeFi (Centralized Finance). Stablecoins are examples of CeFi, and their value equals the central bank currency such as the US dollar. CoinBase is another CeFi that allows people to buy cryptocurrencies, then stores them and lends them in a centralized manner.

Uses of Decentralized Finance

Borrowing and Lending

Open lending protocols are part of the DeFi ecosystem; open borrowing in DeFi has advantages over Traditional systems such as instant transactions, turning digital assets into collateral, and no credit checks to authorize transactions. Lending services are built on blockchains, which reduces counterparty risks as it makes these two services cheaper, faster, and readily available to many people.

Monetary Banking Services

As the blockchain develops, there's a focus towards stable coins as they help to navigate both industries (DeFi and Traditional finance) at the same time. The transfer occurs between tangible life assets and digital assets; for example, in Mortgages and insurance, it reduces transaction fees and the period taken to acquire the goods and eliminates intermediaries. The elimination of communities that have run centralized finance is the smart move that has made DeFi popular among its users worldwide.

Decentralized Marketplaces

This segment offers more room for innovation in DeFi through applications known as Decentralized exchanges (DEXes). These DeFi platforms allow users to trade digital assets directly without an intermediary to hold their assets and funds; they have lower trading fees and exchanges.

DeFi is a new field, and like any other financial market, education on trade is crucial. With education on cryptocurrency, how and where to invest, how to trade and grow wealth, and how crypto markets operate: users will be able to make intelligent decisions as they trade their digital assets. As DeFi moves towards creating a more open financial system, it solves existing problems of government censorship on finances and economic discriminations all over the world.

The Origin of Decentralized Finance

We currently live in a financial era where currencies are used for trading, purchasing goods, and paying for services. For a while now, banks have been a centralized platform that operated all sorts of currencies for the general population. With centralized finance as a monopoly, individuals did not have as much freedom over their finances and assets because of government control. Decentralized finance was created to offer absolute control of assets and personal finances over individuals, whether at a corporate or individual level.

DeFi was created in August 2018 through a telegram chat between Ethereum developers and some entrepreneurs like Inje Yeo of Set protocol, Brendan Forster of Dharma, and Ox Blake Henderson. They discussed options on what to name the movement of open financial applications on Ethereum, and the name DeFi came off as (DEFY) which worked best.

The DeFi timeline can be traced and explained like this. In November 2013, the ethereum project was announced in a paper title "A next-generation Smart Contract and Decentralized Platform" by Vitalik Buterin. In July 2015, the Ethereum blockchain was launched. In December 2017, a significant shift as MarkerDAO was launched, allowing users to do more with their money than basic transactions.

MarkerDAO, an ethereum-based protocol, allowed cryptocurrency trade pegged on the US Dollar. It allowed the borrowing of stablecoins like Dai against Ether, and it created a way to take loans and paved the way for dollar-pegged Digital assets. At the beginning of 2018, the DeFi ecosystem expanded as more Dapps were created and launched on Ethereum; as time went by, it gained more ground online. As of 2021, a new era for DeFi has been set as it expands with more Dapps and new use cases achieved daily.

Characteristics of Decentralized Finance

Non-custodial

These distributed networks allow users to control their assets and finance; any transfer from one person to the other is done independently without intermediaries like banks and financial institutions. Only users hold a right to their private keys and digital wallets and can control their funds.

Open

These networks eliminate financial borders as they operate globally, and anyone has access to DeFi from any point in the world. Finances are transferred seamlessly, faster, and any amount is viable for transfer.

Transparent

The code attached to this system is open to anyone to see and inspect; this is important because a user can verify protocols and how they work and track their money.

Decentralized

DeFi protocols are built on blockchains such as ethereum, and this software is spread and run worldwide, making it almost impossible to be censored. Users take charge of their financial assets and suggest changes to be made while still benefiting from trade.

The Special Things about DeFi

Cryptocurrency will do to banks what emails did to postal services. Traditional finance is on the brink of revolution, this sector has experienced cracks since before the global pandemic, and these loopholes are what DeFi is filling up. Financial independence is a goal everyone works towards, and DeFi has provided a way to do just that as it has become the new trend to watch out for in finance. What is the unique thing about DeFi?

1. Decentralization

This financial space does not have a central government, and for this reason, an individual has direct access to their finances and what their finances can do for them such as trade and acquire assets. These platforms have removed all intermediaries and go-betweens in financial transactions using Smart contracts, and it has increased profits and lowered transaction fees. Any sort of activity conducted on cryptocurrency is permissionless.

2. Stablecoins Advantage

DeFi has found a way to link fiat currencies with cryptocurrency, where crypto is pegged to the US Dollar, creating stablecoins that can be translated into the real world and on digital markets. With stablecoins, one can take instant fiat cash loans using crypto as collateral, which is most advantageous to people in the developing world. DeFi has lowered barriers on retail by offering a high and stable return on investments.

3. Developments into the future

DeFi is making fundamental and fast steps progress into bringing tangible world assets into the blockchain ecosystem. This will encompass individual and corporate entities, which is critical for the future we are headed into. The technology is compelling as it has no liquidity limits, fewer transaction fees, cost-saving, and entirely built on self-interest.

4. Decentralized Applications (Dapps)

Dapps have enabled cryptocurrency trading on Decentralized exchanges (dexs) such as Uniswap that operate as peer-to-peer. DeFi also termed as "Lego money," allows you to stack up dapps together and maximize returns. For example, you can buy Dai stablecoins and trade them on Compound and earn interest; this has impacted day-to-day lives.

5. Privacy

Traditional finance lacks privacy as there are legal requirements, and the borrower knows the lender and vice versa. DeFi is founded on privacy such that there are no public records and operations are based on mutual trust. These trends have governments rethinking a lot of dealings they have on financial matters. In July 2020, the US Securities and Exchange Commission (SEC) made a significant shift concerning DeFi, as they approved Arca, an ethereum based fund.

6. DeFi Tokens

Tokens have brought about the boom on cryptocurrencies experienced in 2020. Tokens are decentralized financial applications that run on blockchains, and the concept runs similarly to fiat currency. They run and operate on Smart Contracts mostly in the ethereum blockchain and eliminate intermediaries. Tokens' main goal is to translate into the real world through stablecoins and taking worldly assets, and translating them into crypto. The tokens for trade are limitless or any platform the market operates for 24 hours a day, all round the clock for the entire year.

Limitations of DeFi

There are disadvantages attached to DeFi that you need to be well acquitted with before you start trading and those that occur in trade. The history of finance has had different limitations; it just depends on the currency at the question. Traditional forms of finance have suffered limitations that have affected individuals, corporate entities, and governments: and DeFi has its share of limitations as well.

1. Uncertainty

The blockchain that hosts DeFi is ethereum, and it is still undergoing some changes in development, to means that it is unstable. As long as the host blockchain is being worked on, any change made affects the DeFi ecosystem. On the other hand, the ethereum version 2.0 that is being developed will hopefully solve this problem.

Attention deficit as protocols with the DeFi governance system increase, it is becoming considerably tricky and time-consuming to keep up with proposed changes.

2. Scalability problem

Scalability in financial institutions means the ability of this institution to handle increased market demands as volumes increases. DeFi has scalability issues associated with the host blockchain. The transactions take longer to be processed hence an increase in transaction costs. The ethereum can process 13 transactions per second compared to other crypto platforms that can process thousands of transactions per second. A bitcoin block size holds at 1 MB, which means it also has limited transactions that will be problematic as transactions increase soon.

3. Smart contract problems

Smart contracts are very vulnerable, and a slight flaw in a smart contract code can lead to loss of funds. Bitcoin DeFi applications are entering the market; since bitcoin is more stable than ethereum, it could solve unstable smart contract problems.

4. Low liquidity

DeFi tokens and blockchain protocols operate on liquidity; this determines the number of users that can benefit. As of October 2020, the total value locked in DeFi is over $12.5 billion; compared to traditional financial systems, this does not match up. Token protocols are highly dependent on traditional finance assets remaining at high valuations, which are not guaranteed.

5. Lack of insurance

Insurance is a critical factor in financial systems as it protects investors from fraud and losses incurred unlawfully. DeFi has close to few insurance policies for its users as compared to traditional financial platforms. DeFi is new, and it has security concerns as no protection is offered from cyberbullying, fraud, losses, and conmen and women, thus making it an insecure trading platform.

6. No law

Generally, there is no standpoint on how legal or illegal cryptocurrency is, and that goes as well for DeFi. There is no governance or code of conduct to situate how and what services and products can be paid and purchased with crypto. In the early days, crypto was linked to terrorist organizations, and because of the decentralized nature of DeFi, there was no paper trail to follow. This could increase illegal activities and crime rates as we advance.

7. Personal faults

There are pros and cons of DeFi; the risks and limitations on these platforms are not responsible for your own mistakes. By nature of being decentralized, responsibilities shift from intermediaries to users; hence, personal losses because of human error are not accounted for by the platform. Personal responsibilities accompany the freedom offered by DeFi, and people are not used to taking care of themselves. Their well-being has been delegated to the government, insurance policies, financial analysts, and advisors; hence, this new field of personal choices and responsibilities may be more complicated than expected to maneuver.

Let us learn the DeFi Lingo.

Since DeFi is relatively new to the market considering the duration it has been around, you must be trying to understand it best you can, but you hit a hard place once in a while because of all the acronyms used. Worry no more; here is the DeFi encyclopedia to help you scan through the information provided to help better your understanding.

AML stands for anti-money laundering that refers to the laws and regulations to prevent criminal activities.

AMM, Automated Market Makers don't work the traditional way buyers, and sellers agree; instead, they interact and trade directly through smart contracts.

Blockchain is a distributed ledger system with a series of blocks that contain verified transactions.

Collateral, this term is used when one is taking loans. The borrower stumps up a percentage of their cryptocurrency to take in a loan, which creates stability in the system.

DAO stands for Decentralized Autonomous Organization, a company that does not have human staff. As an organization, its run by automated machines and has a code that is open source and available to anyone, and it is censorship-resistant.

dApp is a decentralized application that is the foundation of DeFi. It has no human support staff, and it provides a platform for users to transfer funds directly without intermediaries.

DEX/CEX stands for Decentralized exchange and Centralized Exchange, respectively, where you can buy and sell cryptocurrencies and tokens. DEX is run without any human interference through algorithms, while CEX is operated with human management.

Fiat currencies are currencies whose value is decreed by the central bank, and their value is known, e.g., US Dollars or British pound.

Gas fees are charges that ethereum miners receive to process transactions.

The more transactions are going on in the blockchain, the more the gas fees.

Liquidity, also known as Yield Farming, allows users to deposit tokens or cryptocurrency on dApp or DEX for profits. The more you stake, the higher the reward on the farmed crypto.

Liquidity pools are governed by smart contracts and allow people to trade without intermediaries. The Smart Contract government enables the platforms to stay balanced.

NFTs are non-fungible tokens, a significant innovation on the tokens that possess unique characteristics. They are used to buy and sell unique arts and collections and cannot be exchanged for other tokens.

A private key is a string of numbers and letters a user can use to access their digital currency.

Smart Contract is where codes are written, and these codes determine how dApps and other DeFi protocols work in the crypto ecosystem. Once the codes are launched, they cannot be changed by anyone; any bugs they have can lead to them being hacked.

Stablecoins it's the pillar in DeFi, which is a token that reflects traditional currencies. They account for most transactions in DeFi, and it doesn't suffer price volatility.

Tokens are more like company shares on a stock market, but how they operate in the crypto market. Trading them earns profit, although not all tokens are valuable; the most valuable token is ERC-20.

These are just but a few common acronyms, there are more.

Chapter 3: Looking at How DeFi Works

Decentralized Finance uses blockchain technology, and they are public to operate. A blockchain is a type of database, and a database is a collection of information gathered and stored electronically on a computer system. Information or data stored in these databases is stored in a table format that makes it easier to filter needed information. The spreadsheet format is available to individuals and is restricted.

A database houses vast amounts of information that can be accessed, simplified, and customized to fit individual needs simultaneously and by many people. Large databases are built using so many powerful computers, and they host data on servers. They have a high storage capacity that allows access to information simultaneously and to many users at once.

A blockchain as a database collects its information in groups called blocks. Blocks have a storage capacity that, when filled, is chained to a previously filled block creating a chain of data known as blockchains. Because of the block structure and not the usual tables in databases, all blockchains are databases, and not all databases are blockchains. Each block in a chain had a specific timestamp when it was added to the chain.

Blockchains have been used in Bitcoin and Altcoins to store data on every transaction that has taken place. Unlike most databases, the cryptocurrency databases are not housed under the same roof but are owned and operated by individuals separately. The many computers housing Bitcoins information are stored in different geographical locations and are called nodes; thus, they are used in a decentralized manner.

If one node in the bitcoin timestamp has a problem, it can use the other nodes as reference points to correct itself. The information remains the same in all nodes; that is why any transaction made is irreversible; these structures make blockchains so transparent.

Transparency and Security

Due to decentralized Finance, transactions can be viewed by having a remote node through blockchain explorers. Blockchain technology promotes trust and security in several ways:

Blocks are added chronologically at the end of an existing blockchain.

Information stored is not easy to change or reverse unless a majority consensus is reached because it stores its information in timestamps.

Hacking into these blockchains does not survive the test of the day because when other blocks are cross-referenced, the hacked block stands out, and it is cast out immediately. For a hack to be successful, a hacker has to control more than 51% of the blocks.

Smart Contract used in DeFi is a code built into a blockchain to help facilitate and negotiate contract agreements. They operate under a set of conditions between users who borrow or lend in the DeFi platform, and once these conditions are met, the task is carried out automatically.

Advantages and Disadvantages of Blockchain

Advantages

Accuracy of the chain.

The blockchain network removes all human involvement in the verification process as it is run by computers hence avoiding human error. Even if an error occurred, it would be on one block, and the rest of the blocks would help to correct it

Decentralized

Blockchain codes are copied and spread across computer networks and are not stored in a central place. Any time a new block is added, it is reflected on other existing blocks; it becomes challenging to tamper with due to this spread of information.

Cost Reductions

DeFi has eliminated traditional financial processes such as human signature, bank verification, and the duration to process finances. With this, the costs of transactions have been reduced.

Efficient and Private transactions

Transactions under blockchain are processed 24 hours a day all around the year. They are favorable for cross-border transactions which take less than

10 minutes to execute. In as much as blockchain networks operate as public entities, users making these transactions are not made public promoting privacy.

Banking the Unbanked

DeFi, in association with Blockchains, is available to anyone worldwide regardless of their race, economic status, and nationality. Developing countries have benefited from this the most.

Disadvantages

Technology cost

Despite the reduction in transaction fees, technological costs are not free. Electricity bills, internet costs, and hardware expenses are additional costs a user has to bear.

Speed inefficiency

The blockchain network can only process about 7 to 10 transactions per second, which is a limitation as transactions are on the rise as more people pick on cryptocurrencies.

Illegal Activity

DeFi allows for illegal trading activities as it's decentralized and private. Silk Road, a dark web platform selling drugs, was operating with crypto. Financial freedom also allows the same freedoms to criminals.

Five Key Elements in This Ecosystem

There are crucial elements that make up the DeFi ecosystem, and these factors work together to create an environment DeFi thrives in.

Open Ledger Standards

Most of the companies operating under DeFi use open ledger systems once a new kind of DeFi application is developed. A ledger is not under one individual control but has multiple individual participants. Information is passed through the ledgers, and no single entity can authorize it. For compatibility purposes in the ecosystem, common standards ledgers are used.

Open ledgers also offer help to lending platforms with more flexibility as they come encompassed with these benefits; they help make transactions fast, offer transparency, are permissionless, and cannot quickly be censored. These systems eliminated intermediaries in trade and enabled individuals to take ownership of their finances.

Bitcoin and Ethereum are examples of coins operating under permissionless ledgers; it means anyone can join, there's no central owner, proof-of-work is required as a consensus for trade, and pseudonyms protect the user's identity.

Smart Contracts

Smart contracts are programs written under the distributed ledgers that are automatically executed by nodes on the network. Smart Contracts are crucial as they are used to automate orders from lending to borrowing and insurance claims in the ecosystem. Compared to traditional contracts, smart contracts are more favorable as they have eliminated intermediaries and extra costs.

Any instruction that a computer can execute on the DeFi ecosystem can quickly be done through Smart Contracts. Several DAOs (Decentralized Autonomous Organizations) hosted on the ethereum blockchain thrive on codifying rules, decisions, eliminating government by people, and a need for documents for verification.

Stablecoins

Stablecoins are cryptocurrencies that derive their market value from external references. Cryptos are very volatile, and fiat currency is very rigid; a stablecoin comes in between them, which means a reserve asset backs them up; this factor enables them to maintain their price value and avoid volatility.

Cryptocurrency is very volatile, and it brings about uncertainty rendering it unfit for use daily. Stablecoins are pegged against real-world currencies like US Dollars, which, therefore, stabilizes the crypto ecosystem. Stablecoins come in four categories:

• Fiat-collateralized stablecoins are backed up by a fiat currency such as a pound or a dollar. They are pegged on a racial of 1:1 such cryptocurrencies include TrueUSD and tether (USDT).

• Crypto-collateralized stablecoins are pegged against another cryptocurrency, they are highly volatile, and their ratio isn't 1:1. They are over-collateralized to means a high number of crypto is pumped in to withstand volatility and fluctuations.

● Commodity-collateralized stablecoins are backed by commodities such as silver or gold and real estate, oil, and precious metals.

● Any reserve asset does not back Non-collateralized (Algorithmic) stablecoins; their value is used to maintain stability in the ecosystem, just like the central bank uses the US Dollar to maintain stability on Fiat currencies.

Marketplaces and Exchanges

Decentralized and open markets are part of DeFi, these are places one can buy and trade their goods using cryptocurrency, and their privacy is maintained. They are favorable because of reduced costs of transactions and the variety of products and services one can purchase. These are the online platforms where you can use your coins to better areas of your life.

Uniswap developed AMM (Automated Market making) that provided prices for the liquidity pool. It sets a price for products and services in these marketplaces so that the decision isn't left entirely to the buyers and sellers. Uniswap is a win for the decentralized ecosystem as it is the place used to compete against centralized alternatives.

Asset Management and Insurance platforms

The DeFi ecosystem covers asset management and insurance platforms, which give individuals the power to control their investment opportunities. Crypto assets are insured just in case of a system error; the user is refunded the losses they have incurred. Smart Contracts are used to work out management and insurance and the authenticity of each claim.

The Biggest Defi in the Market

Uniswap is the most sought-after crypto exchange and a gateway to quick riches in the DeFi ecosystem. It operates on the ethereum blockchain and promotes peer-to-peer transactions. According to CoinMarketCap.com, a data tracker Uniswap daily average trading volume lies at around $220 million. Uniswap platform houses crypto strategies such as Yield Farming, the most profitable factor supporting lending and pooling cryptocurrencies in exchange for fees and interests.

Uniswap doesn't require identity verification from their users to allow them to own tokens and generate revenues, unlike other traditional crypto exchanges that started to bow down to regulatory pressures to curb illicit activities, especially money laundering. The Uniswap platform is decentralized and allows users to trade without intermediaries, and one can swap ERC-20 tokens for another directly.

In an attempt to solve a "vampire attack" from SushiSwap in 2020, Uniswap created 400 tokens and gave them to around 250,000 wallet owners in the platform, and its value went up again. Social media platforms such as Twitter have been used for advertising Uniswap by some financially influential people that contributed to its surge rise in market value.

The AMM technology under Smart contracts is what makes Uniswap work efficiently. When a transaction is made, the AMM algorithm decides on the proper token for that trade. The platform charges a 0.3% transaction fee; when the fees are added together, they are used to reward any user who contributes to the liquidity pool.

Uniswap introduced UNI, a token used in governance in September 2020, and any user who holds a UNI token can vote and make changes on the trajectory evolution on the platform. The UNI holders use this token to fund grants, liquidity pools, and partnerships and decisions that grow the DeFi community.

DeFi and Other Currencies

DeFi operates with other currencies, among them Ethereum; DeFi applications (dApps) are built on the ethereum blockchain. Under this, we have Decentralized Exchange (DEXs), a platform where trade occurs both in buying, selling, lending, and borrowing. Payment services and acquisition services happen on peer-to-peer platforms without intermediaries.

Decentralized Finance is also available in Bitcoin and Altcoins that form different tokens apart from uniswap. They operate on tokens like Sushiswap that operate similarly to Uniswap when the cloned code was made operational at some point.

The majority of DeFi protocols have been customized to work with ethereum; others have been split into other coins, for example, Bitcoin Cash, a sub-branch coin of bitcoin. DeFi start-ups have been raising funds needed in the hopes of taking the DeFi sector on platforms other than that of ethereum. Of the 232 registered DeFi projects, 214 of them are built on ethereum.

Marker, a token of governance for the MarkerDao, launched major automated crypto-lending platforms in the ecosystem in 2017. Marker manages DAI; a cryptocurrency pegged to the US Dollar. The marker token gives governance power on the voting rights to borrow and lend on the DAI stablecoin.

Compound currency has compound pools run on a decentralized platform that enables users to earn interest by depositing their token coins in any pool. In June 2020, compound launched its coin after operating on ethereum for a while. It's called COMP. The compound is run on algorithms, and their interest rate protocols are built for developers.

Other DeFi currencies are in the market, like Aave, which runs on the AAVE token. Synthetix, whose native token is SNX; a user is required to stake about 750% of synths to value in SNX. YEarn running on a native token YFI offers a liquidity pool for yield farming opportunities.

DeFi tokens operating on different cryptocurrencies offer opportunities in the permissionless ecosystem to make profits. There are many operational currencies on DeFi, but the leading one is on Ethereum.

Assuring Your Security

DeFi platforms are as safe as the codes they run on. DeFi would represent the evolution of the promise Bitcoin was built on more than a decade ago. DeFi platforms have shown promise in being more secure than centralized finance platforms, but it doesn't come without its challenges and shortcomings.

Stolen codes and re-entrance attacks are happening more frequently on these platforms. Since the DeFi ecosystem operates on blockchains, it would be a bit more challenging to hack the entire system, but it is doable. The DeFi ecosystem is in its early stages, and proper protocols need to be put in place to curb insecurities in the platforms. Here are some risks experienced in DeFi and how to curb them:

Technical risks

These risks arise from the software codes and protocols running DeFi platforms. In a technical error occurrence on blockchains, it could jeopardize the entire chain and its functions. Factors in technical risks include memory safety and race conditions, which affect the results of a transaction. Developers should conduct proper testing on codes before they are made operational, and as a user, do your research and choose the most stable DeFi system.

Smart Contract, Hardware, and Software Risks

Timestamp dependence on Smart Contracts is a vulnerability loophole targeted by hackers, and also a change or delay in a timestamp affects the whole chain and delays transactions. Power issues like electricity are a hardware risk that can lead to data loss because this DeFi is computerized, and the machines run on power. Each attack faced has revealed developmental problems on these three fronts.

Financial risks

This often comes as an individual risk to the user, and an investor cannot reverse wrong transactions. Its liquidity is relatively still small to maintain a high market demand; a more extensive market must meet the demand.

Procedural risks

It starts when hackers manipulate and copy a code and lure unsuspecting users into trading on that platform. Personal and sensitive information is then leveraged against the user when trading; cyberbullying and hackers can use their provided information to commit illegal activities.

Regulatory risks

DeFi operates in traditional arenas that have oversight from governments and worldwide regulatory bodies. Due to the permissionless Claus in DeFi, there are regulatory concerns that criminals could use this body for illegal purposes. It is not fully equipped against fraud, scams, and illegal transactions.

How to secure yourself against DeFi Risks

- Do the research and use trustworthy services and products, go through reviews, and make the best decision on how to proceed forward.

- Create a multi-factor authentication password on your digital wallet, trading platforms, and email account.

- Keep your digital assets private to ward off thieves and hackers, don't share your personal trading information with anyone.

- Secure all your digital assets by insuring them; hot storage is critical as one accesses their DeFi services and cold storage for accessing data when offline.

- Smart Contract audits should be incorporated by management to help with keeping the platforms secure by foreshadowing threats before they occur.

- The DeFi ecosystem requires more awareness of its run, its aspects, the risks and threats it faces. This will help users invest in a platform they are fully aware of, and also, the management could be more aware of bugs in the systems that need fixing.

In its early stages, DeFi has shown promise to be the future of modern finance. Clearly, work needs to be done to improve the quality, liquidity in the market, and concerns from the users. After the pandemic, the value of DeFi has skyrocketed as investors worldwide were figuring new ways to make money. Outside of the technical issues, Decentralized Finance has what it takes to create a global financial decentralized system and blockchain developers are working to fix this problem. The future of finance lies in DeFi.

Section 2: Getting into the Investment

Chapter 4 - Dive into Stablecoins

The Concept of Stablecoins

A stablecoin is a cryptocurrency whose value is pegged to a reserve asset such as the US Dollar, gold, or other unique metals, in an attempt to create price stability. Cryptocurrencies offer digital trading to buy goods and services and pay for them using Bitcoin or Altcoins. Still, there is a setback: cryptocurrencies are highly volatile, and their prices keep fluctuating.

Cryptocurrencies, especially Bitcoin and Ethereum's unpredictability, gives fiat currencies an edge over crypto in the real world. Fiat currencies can maintain daily transactions that crypto cannot, and this led to the need and creation of stablecoins that tackle these price fluctuations in the ecosystem. Fiat currencies are government-issued currencies, stablecoins work on a ratio of 1:1, and for example, $1 million US dollars is pegged against 1 million units of the stablecoin.

Stablecoin creates a reserve and stores the assets backing up the stablecoin; these digital stablecoins are tied to real-world assets. The currency in reserve serves as collateral, and a user can redeem one unit of stablecoin for one unit of the assets it backs, be it gold or cash. Stablecoins get more complex as they are backed and collateralized by other cryptocurrencies.

Stablecoins are collateralized with the following assets to create balance;

• Fiat currencies – are the most common collateral for stable coins. The US Dollar is the most pegged currency, and currently, Bilira is pegged to the Turkish Lira. The reserves created by fiat collaterals are maintained by independent custodians who are regularly audited.

• Commodity-based stablecoins are tied to Precious metals that include silver and gold, among others.

● Non-collateralized stablecoins do not have any reserve assets; their stability is derived from similar working mechanisms like those of the central bank.

● Cryptocurrencies are pegged against each other like ether an ethereum token works as collateral. Due to high volatility, such stablecoins are over-collateralized.

Popular Stablecoins

Diem

Stablecoin, formally known as Libra developed by Facebook, is yet to be launched but had quite a significant take in than any other coin. Governments like China are working to create their inspiring cryptocurrencies because they could have global users. After all, Diem is owned by a popular platform. Diem is working to create multiple stablecoins backed by different currencies.

Tether

It was launched in 2014; it is the most valuable and popular stablecoin in the crypto market. It balances currencies and has beneficial advantages when it comes to trade and profits.

USD Coin

Stablecoin launched in 2018 and is managed jointly by Coinbase and circle firms through a center consortium.

Dai

It runs on MarkerDAO protocol on the ethereum blockchains. A plan is underway to make DAI a decentralized Stablecoin to means no one can own or control it.

There are several risks involved in trading using stablecoins; this chapter will discuss them at great length.

How Stable are Stablecoins

Unstable stablecoins are an oxymoron because they are not as solid stable as many investors think—stablecoins aim at fixing the volatility problems that come with cryptocurrencies to work out payment issues.

Stablecoins are as stable as the underlying asset.

The stability of the pegged asset determines how stable a stablecoin is going to be. Trade volumes have stablecoins deviating in worth from their underlying assets. Twenty-four stablecoins have failed so far; 16 of them were pegged to gold. Gold is more volatile, and it is highly subjected to price fluctuation and the value of the gold effect. Gold custody is also another challenge. If a stablecoin is pegged to any currency, any slight effect on that currency affects the stability of the stablecoin by inflation or deflation.

Stablecoin Investors

Investors need to be aware of how volatile stablecoins are, and they are not fully decentralized. The assets put in collateral are put under the custody of a person; hence, investors rely on a private management company. As an investor, you need to do studies and research on how stable an underlying asset is? And how trustworthy is the issuing entity?

Crypto-collateral Safety

As far are these stablecoins are concerned, they suffer several risks because of technological risks like being hacked, computer malfunctions, and data loss. There is a risk of volatility as prices fall too much and too quickly, making them unreliable. The stability of bitcoin and Altcoins needs to be addressed to keep these ecosystems afloat.

In the general cryptocurrency market, currencies are highly volatile, and stablecoins are the most stable coins. A few issues need to be worked on to stabilize them even further, but this is as stable as it gets in the DeFi system.

Stablecoin insurance has played a role in creating specific stability enjoyed by traditional systems of finance. Stablecoin premiums and discounts contribute to a more stable market as they provide a hedge for non-stable crypto assets.

Developers should improve the sources of instability in stablecoins such as high return correlation, volatility, and high trading volume correlation to Bitcoin to create more stability in the stablecoins to make them as stable as fiat currencies.

The Three Kinds of Stablecoins

There are three types of stablecoins and include Fiat-Centralized stablecoins, Crypto-centralized stablecoins, and Non-collateralized stablecoins. A fourth unique stablecoin is the Commodity Centralized coin. Here is a deeper understanding.

Fiat Centralized Stablecoins

Centralized IOU stablecoins are backed with Fiat currencies such as the US Dollars or any other sovereign currency. These stablecoins have a centralized nature, a criticism that has been expressed in the DeFi ecosystem as fiat currencies fully back them. The centralized structure operates on a degree of trust through third-party auditing. Categories of fiat centralized Stablecoins include:

TrueUSD (TUSD) was launched in March 2018 by TrustToken, a company specializing in traditional assets tokenization. The platform is very transparent as it publishes bank accounts content daily and has monthly audits.

Gemini launched Gemini Dollar alongside PAX tokens launched by Paxos. The US Dollar collateralizes both tokens on a ratio of 1:1. They were both licensed in 2015, and they comply with regulations such that governments can seize them in case of use in illegal activities.

Their general advantages are; they are simple and straightforward to understand. Their stability is almost sure because fiat currencies back them. Disadvantages are that they are centralized, making them prone to failure, bankruptcy, and moral hazards. Their requirement of trust goes against cryptocurrencys` principles since they allow external audits. Regulations and oversight could compromise their efficiency and conversion process.

Crypto-collateralized Stablecoins

Digital assets back these stablecoins on blockchains; this stablecoin operates by being collateralized with another crypto asset such as Ethereum or other tokens. They include:

DAI stablecoin hosted by MarkerDAO has a two-coin model, the marker coin (MKR) and DAI. Dai as a stablecoin is helpful as you can lock ether in

Collateralized debt positions (CDP).

Havven also features a two-coin model nomins (nUSD) and Havven (HAV). Nominees have a floating supply, stabilizing the price, while havven has a stable supply that provides collateral for the system. The stability of nomins heavily relies on the market value of Havven, and Havens over collateralizes the system.

It has several advantages such as decentralization, this promotes transparency, and its liquidation is very efficient as it is crypto to crypto. It is disadvantaged due to high volatility, they are complex to mine, and its price value falls below the standard threshold because of instant liquidation.

Non-Collateralized Stablecoins

Senior shares are how non-collateralized stablecoins operate; this is by mimicking the central bank, but on digital assets, new coins are issued by the network and thrive on the price market value. Examples are:

Basis token is stabilized through on-chain supply management. When the value of the basis is not at equilibrium, the Smart Contract either increases or decreases the supply and brings the price back to $1. This works by burning coins or increasing the supply to balance the market.

CarbonUSD began as a fiat-collateralized stablecoin with a plan to eventually switch to hybrid fiat algorithmic model, and it is currently using the ethereum blockchain.

They are advantaged because they are decentralized; they are stable because their value is constantly adjusted to suit the market and the absence of collaterals. However, they are very complex and, at times, challenging to comprehend.

Commodity based stablecoin

This category of stablecoins has the backing of commodities. Commodities are assets that are interchanged for purposes of trade; the common commodity collateralized is gold and precious metals. Gold has been viewed as a good store of value considering other assets, the gold asset is stored at a third party, and the ratio operates as 1:1. There are also commodities backed by oil, such as Petro coin, backed by Venezuela's oil reserves.

They operate at an advantage because tangible assets back them with real value that promotes real assets in the world. They are relatively stable, and they bring significant liquidity to the crypto market. On the other hand, they are disadvantaged because they are centralized and require to be audited, which is expensive and time-consuming.

Tether makes 98% of the market trade-in stablecoins; every stablecoin developed after that looks to level up to tether. Increased demand for one of the four categorized stablecoins leads to the growth of the cryptocurrency market hence strengthening Decentralized Finance.

Digix gold tokens (dgx) are an ERC-20 token backed by gold fully audited and stored in a Singapore vault. Each token's value depends on the market value of gold, and it is audited every three months.

Importance of Stablecoins

Without a plan to stick around for the future, there is no use to adopt cryptocurrency because it will be risky. The formation of stablecoins fixed this market worry for all the investors, and they play these crucial roles.

Alleviate political and economic hardship developing countries benefit from this advantage as they live in countries with high inflation rates, which reduces purchasing power. In the past, this has resulted in political and economic uncertainties. An example is Venezuela; its fiat currency was undervalued by 95%. The government-imposed laws make it hard to move the capital elsewhere and preserve its value. Stablecoins ensure that currencies are preserved and solve political and economic fallout.

Hedging mechanism for traders reduces adverse price movements in purchasing or selling assets or services. Stablecoins are used in the crypto market as a hedge to Altcoins and Bitcoin. It has become a solution for the procedures used in traditional finance.

Meet the Most Popular Stablecoins

Like fiat currencies that differ in value worldwide, so do stablecoins; some are more stable and profitable than others. In the book, we have covered some of them; let's have a final look that is more detailed.

Tether USDT

Just as its name suggests, it tethers itself to the US Dollar, and it is the most well-known stable coin in the crypto market. Tether is backed by gold, fiat currencies, and cash equivalents—about 94% of the stablecoin trading volume. USDT works on an ethereum blockchain and helps its investors and users track their investments without bitcoin.

Tether is not audited like the other centralized stablecoins; because of this, lawsuits have been filed against its parent company BitFinex and nothing has been done against it so far.

USD Coin (USDC)

It is a stablecoin backed by CoinBase, the largest holder and bitcoin broker worldwide. It runs on ethereum, stella, and Solana blockchains, and was launched in 2018. Its pegged to the value of the US Dollar.

Diem

Diem is a facebook backed stablecoin that is yet to be released to the market. It runs on a Diem blockchain, and its wallet is called Novi; it is programmable to allow the creation of apps. It has validator nodes that are used to confirm transactions and validate blocks. Its blockchain aims to enable 1000 transactions per second with near to zero transaction fees.

DAI

Ethereum developers formulated the MarkerDAO project to fix fluctuation problems in DeFi through a stablecoin called DAI. This stablecoin is pegged to the US Dollar; it offers stabilization and transparency considering it is built on the ethereum network. DAI is kept stabilized through a series of Centralized Debt Positions (CDPs) that are Smart Contracts built on the ethereum blockchain.

Users can do just about anything with DAI, including putting it on a personal savings account, making payments and investments. Since DAI is pegged on the US Dollar, every loan is paid back with interests. Target Rate Feedback Mechanism (TRFM) is an automatic Mechanism used by DAI to remain stable. TRFM and Target rate in DAI is determined by how dynamic the market supply is, which works on a real-time basis.

Gold coin

It is a stablecoin backed by gold, and it's built on the Ethereum platform. The cryptocurrency allows you to buy gold in little bits, and it is stored for you by a third party in secure volts. After the complete purchase of a certain amount of gold, it can be shipped to you once you provide proof of trade and ownership.

Paxos Standard Token (PAX)

It is backed by the United States Dollar and was created alongside tether. It is built on the ethereum platform and approved by the New York States Department of Financial Services. This posits it to be more trustworthy than USDT.

Binance USD (BUSD)

The stablecoin is backed by a Binance exchange that is ethereum based with the US dollar's fiat backing. It is held in FDIC-insured banks in the US and used to pay for trading and exchange fees.

Risks Involved

Hacks and Exploits

How secure a protocol code determines the security of the funds locked in DeFi. One risk of a booming technology is the rush by developers to get on a trend, which leaves bugs on blockchains that can be exploited and hacked. Scams are also part of risks as rogue actors place fake tokens on legit platforms that do not amount to any real value, which frustrates the users. Before a blockchain is released to the market, the developers should ensure all the bugs are fixed. It is an individual responsibility to take care of personal gadgets and step up security on them.

Ethereum Dominance

There's an issue of scalability to deal with; DeFi ecosystems are built on ethereum, ethereum classic, and bitcoin cash. The dominance of ethereum makes it not possible to scale the blockchain and meet growing industry needs. The platform is yet to implement a fulfilling scaling solution, and developers are working on multiple ways to accommodate future growth.

Gas Costs

Every transaction requires gas to process, and calculating the cost of that gas is a bit challenging. If the gas price used is too low, then the transaction may not go through, and if it's too high, the user may end up spending more than planned. Do your research and learn how to calculate the cost of the trade before you make a transaction.

Risks with Loans

Borrowing and lending loans come with risks; some lending protocols like Aave require a user to put up collateral. If one may be under collateralized, the user adds more funds to avoid liquidation, which is expensive.

Financial risks

Price volatility puts the users' investments at the risk of losing everything. When trading, one stands a chance to lose all their liquidated assets; using stablecoins can help navigate these risks.

Losing control over your assets

There are many ways an investor can lose control over their crypto assets, and this includes misplacing private keys and your digital wallet. On the other hand, crypto platforms can shut down and disappear with the client's investments. One is recommended to use a non-custodial wallet which means you are the only one with control over your assets.

With proper development, stablecoins could be the new currency as we live in the technological era. They operate just like Fiat currencies; the difference is the platform; however, their value and legality remain subjects to risks, volatility, and market fluctuations. In its early stages, stablecoins have proven to be the future of finance; when their value gets pegged to multiple fiat currencies, their worth and availability will skyrocket.

There are more stablecoins in the DeFi ecosystem, and more are being developed daily.

Chapter 5 - Putting in the Money

Cryptocurrency has become the digital substitute to conventional exchange methods such as credit cards or cash. Different individuals have varying opinions about the digital option. The school of thought views cryptocurrency as a monetary platform for radicals and swindlers involved in Crypto Trojan scams and dark web exchanges.

However, the latest upsurge in Bitcoin's value has proven crypto as a worthwhile investment. This establishment has been backed up by the positive buildup surrounding Blockchain technology. The hype is that blockchain technology powers wallets and the exchange practices of traders in the world. For an individual to successfully invest in cryptocurrency, they have to understand the following main concepts:

First Things First

Rewards of Investing in Cryptocurrency

Transactions

The traditional dealings involve brokers, agents, and senates who make the process complicated and more expensive. There are also intermediary costs, filing, commissions, and other specific conditions which can apply. Cryptocurrency transactions offer direct dealings which occur in a P2P networking structure. The procedure gives more transparency when launching audit trails and accountability since the two participants know their identities.

Asset Transfers

A particular financial analyst says that cryptocurrency resembles a "big property privileges database." The "database" at one point can perform and implement two-part contracts on products such as automobiles and real estate. On another level, it can facilitate unique transfer modes. Since cryptocurrency owners have total control of their accounts, the period and costs involved in asset transference are minimized.

More Conditional Transactions

Each deal an individual makes is an exclusive interchange between the two participants. The negotiation and agreeing terms are confidential to the two individuals. Data interchange is done on a "push" basis where individuals point out precisely what they need the recipient to get. This prevents other parties from accessing the individual's monetary history and reduces account dangers. The process is more confidential than in a conventional system, where an individual's data may be leaked at any point during the deal.

More Credit Accessibility

Digital information transference and the net facilitates the interchange process in crypto. The services are easily accessible to any individual with a data link. The Medias also provide cryptocurrency knowledge for free, and their web pages and portals are easily accessible. There are approximately two billion people globally with data connections but no access to conventional systems of interchange. The cryptocurrency network can make asset transference and deal accessible by these individuals. This can be possible once the necessary digital and monitoring infrastructures are implemented.

Easier International Trade

Cryptocurrencies are not subjected to interchange and interest rates, transaction fees, or other costs imposed by a particular nation. Moreover, the P2P mechanism provides a medium where overseas transferences and trades can be conducted with no currency interchange fluctuations.

Give Me A Sign!

Factors to Consider Before Investing in Cryptocurrency

- **Best Use of the Money**

An individual looking for the right moment to invest in Cryptocurrencies should first determine the best usage for that money. For example, an individual with a bank loan should consider paying the loan first. The consideration is because the interest charged can cause the loan to be more than the returns they get after investing. One can also buy insurance before investing. The insurance protects investors from monetary catastrophes that can clear all their capital or put them into colossal debt when they occur.

- **Investing Objective**

What is your aim? Confident investors may want to grow their capital fast without caring about the risk. Such people have plenty of time to pick themselves up and recover from the losses if they occur. Other traders aim at preserving their money most safely because they will require the money soon, and no loss should occur. The varying objectives are well-suited with diverse methods of investing. Therefore, an individual should research to determine which method fits them best. One can also capitalize for diverse aims; for the short term, one can invest for a house down disbursement, and for the long term, one can invest to retire.

- **Age**

A younger investor has more time to wait for their investment to give returns. The individuals are more secure since they have fewer responsibilities, more disposable earning, and can quickly recover from a loss. Therefore, younger investors can engage in more risky investments that can potentially give them returns above average. However, middle-aged individuals who are thinking of retirement should invest the maximum capital that they can afford. Such investors should consider putting their capital in safer investments to minimize the risk of losing much before they retire. Individuals can follow the "120 minus your age" formula to determine the percentage of stock they should hold.

- **Period before Needing the Cash**

Not every individual capitalizes on retiring since others invest for short-term goals. An individual should consider the time they have before turning the investments into cash. Long-term investments enable an individual to take more risks and hopefully get more gains; have time to recover from potential losses. An investor who does not have plenty of time should engage in less risky investments such as bonds. One should also know that some investments have penalties if redeemed before the holding period is over. One should also put into consideration the tax implications that come with investment withdrawal.

- **Risk Tolerance**

The riskier the investment, the higher the potential return. However, not every individual can risk their money to certain levels. Not everyone is convenient with the upwards and downwards movements of the marketplace. For example, staking your cash in the hope of a higher profit might not be worth losing sleep and anxiety. Investors who can accommodate losing cash for the hope of receiving more profits should engage in aggressive investments like growth stocks. Conservative investors should select safer investments such as bonds.

Four Elements That You Should Understand

Fiat-to-Crypto Exchange

Fiat to crypto interchange helps many new traders. Most Beginners experience hardships when thinking out how to change their fiat coinage, USD, to digital coinage, Bitcoin. The exchange has several roles. The exchanges permit an individual to use conventional disbursement ways when making their original purchase of crypto. The traditional methods include credit and debit cards or bank accounts. Some crypto exchanges only permit the withdrawal and deposition of crypto sums of money but not fiat coins. The exchanges are also accessible when one wants to change the crypto to fiat coinage.

Options to Choose From:

● The coinbase - Known to be a safe crypto exchange in the industry. Means of disbursement accepted include debit and credit cards or bank and wire transfers. The cards are the swiftest technique of changing fiat to Crypto in Coinbase. Moreover, an individual's identification is required while using Coinbase.

● Binance - They are the most recommended exchange. Gives a variety of swapping pairs for any genuine interchange. Binance allows cards, debit and credit, money, and wire transferences as disbursement means. Identity authentication is needed when using Binance.

● Changelly - An individual is not required to identify themselves while performing crypto to crypto swapping. However, identity authentication is needed when purchasing crypto with fiat coinage. Methods of disbursement allowed include cards, credit and debit, and bank transferences. Credit and debit card payouts are faster but at higher pay, whereas bank transferences are slower with lower pay.

● eToro- They offer both traditional investment alternatives and fiat to crypto interchanges. They permit debit and credit cards or wire transferences as their methods of disbursement—an individual needs to authenticate themselves before carrying the transactions.

Crypto-Wallet

It is an app that allows crypto users to keep and retrieve their digital assets. Crypto wallet helps an individual to store their cash in one place. Nakamoto launched the initial crypto wallet during the first release of Bitcoin in 2009. The wallet can store multiple cryptocurrencies, Bitcoin, and all those buildings on its blockchain technology. When individuals want to acquire crypto, they should direct the sender to an exclusive cryptocurrency address given by the wallet. One can view cryptocurrency in their wallet as one can view files in a drive.

Role in Cryptocurrency Transactions

Consents individuals to keep their cryptocurrencies. Moreover, a trader can manage the balance of dual cryptocurrencies such as BTC and ETH. The wallet also allows a person to access their wallet by downloading the mobile application or logging into the Blockchain website.

Options to Select From

● Hot wallets

● Web wallets

● Mobile wallets

- Cold wallets

- Hardware wallets

Crypto-to-Crypto Exchange

The interchange platform allows an individual to change from one Cryptocurrency, Bitcoin, to another, such as Ethereum. The exchange also provides liquidity in three varying levels. The liquidity levels include asset, exchange, and market liquidities.

Role in Cryptocurrency Transactions

The interchange platform plays several roles in the cryptocurrency universe:

❑ It offers transparency and accountability to crypto investors.

❑ It provides better security for crypto by providing a reliable store of values.

❑ It provides a long-term appreciation potential.

Options to Select From:

- FTX - Available for individuals who want to take advantage of digital coinages with leverage. The platform offers various indicators and leveraged indexes that can be swapped on futures and alternative markets. Index futures can be swapped straight from the interchange platform.

● Kraken - It is a top-five exchange platform. This is due to its traffic, swapping magnitudes, and liquidity. Kraken has about fifty crypto assets accessible for purchasing and selling. The assets include Bitcoin, Ethereum, and DeFi indexes such as Compound and Kava. An individual using this platform can scrutinize the marketplace and control their portfolio using one interface.

Crypto Banks

The banks involve cryptocurrency banking and asset applications. The applications permit an individual to have secure purchasing, retailing, and holding of digital assets; their role. The banks not only have crypto wallets, but they also have federally-covered bank accounts and debit cards paid in advance. The cryptocurrency banking services are customarily controlled. The conventional financial universe is emerging with the new universe of cryptocurrencies hence the increase of crypto banks.

Options to Select From:

● CEX.IO - It is an online market. An individual can purchase or sell cryptocurrencies on this platform. One can also swap crypto assets or exchange them for fiat cash.

● Block - The account allows the trader to earn interest in their crypto. One can also borrow cash against it and purchase or retail cryptocurrencies.

● Nexo- One can also borrow against their crypto holdings or swap crypto and fiat. Moreover, a trader can buy Nexo tokens which allows them to earn dividends.

● Crypto.com - It is a cryptocurrency interchange. It allows an individual to purchase or sell crypto that pays interest. Besides, it offers credit against crypto and reward cards.

In the Process of Purchasing

Step-by-Step Guide in Purchasing Cryptocurrencies

What is your aim? Some investors need to acquire profits from their crypto while holding. Others require more interest than what banking gives. Decentralized Finance; Defi is a cryptocurrency drive that generates an optional monetary system that aids medium investors from being exploited by experienced investors and banking directors. These four crucial concepts that an individual should comprehend before purchasing cryptocurrencies:

Purchasing from Fiat to Crypto

An individual is required to purchase cryptocurrency using their fiat currency, such as USD. The process should occur in the Fiat-to-Crypto interchanges. Many interchange platforms are safe and covered; hence, individuals should select an exchange that best suits them. Some aspects that investors may consider; ease to use, dealing fees, and several cryptocurrencies accessible for purchase. The Fiat-to-Crypto interchanges consist of a limited quantity of crypto for free because of supervisory necessities. Crypto-to-Crypto interchanges permit an individual to access a variety of crypto since their regulation is minimum.

Tip: One can use Coinbase as their fiat-to-crypto interchange. The coin gives one a safe, intuitive, straightforward, covered, and managed platform at lower costs. Coinbase conducts plenty of studies before it can permit crypto to be bought on its interchange. This guarantees the investor that the crypto being sold has incredible commercial proposals and isn't a fraud. Moreover, Coinbase provides accessibility to Coinbase Pro as the Crypto-to-Crypto interchange.

Getting a Wallet

An individual should then generate a Crypto-Wallet. The software wallets provide a speedy means of storing cryptocurrencies. The holder can be generated quickly; click "Generate Fresh Wallet" and choose a twelve-alphabet retrieval sentence. After creating the wallet, one can move crypto coinages from their crypto interchange account like Coinbase to their holder address. The holder's address consists of thirty-two to forty alphanumeric typescripts. One can "cut" and "paste" their holder address from the app to the interchange account. The individual should write down the recovery phrase to avoid losing their cryptocurrencies if they forget it. An investor can select a Single coin holder when investing in a particular Crypto like Ethereum. However, if they desire to invest in different Cryptocurrencies, they should choose multi-coin holders.

Tip: One can use Coinbase, Trust, and Metamask Holders. Coinbase is a straightforward and steady multi-coin application that gives an individual, uninterrupted access to DApps. MetaMask is an extension of the browser and allows a trader to link to crypto interchanges and other DApps easily. Trust wallet has plenty of aspects unavailable in Coinbase and MetaMask. Such features include; capability to stake crypto coinages such as Tron to produce Stake Prizes and Wallet Link when linking to Dapps. The Wallet Connect is more steady and effective in contrast to Coinbase's Holder Link.

Transferring the Crypto to Your Wallet

An individual should first extract the wallet address of the crypto they want to transfer in. One should first "cut" and "paste" the wallet address in the "Recipient" and then choose the amount of crypto they want to send. The "Network fee" in the authentication window indicates the fee required for the deal to go through. Unlike the bank, the fee charged depends on network traffic, which charges per the amount being transferred.

Tip: One should note that if they transfer one Crypto like Bitcoin to another Crypto like Ethereum, they will lose their crypto. For example, Bitcoin should be sent to the Bitcoin wallet address and Ethereum to the Ethereum wallet address. Besides, the trader should always ensure they have some quantity of cryptocurrencies to cater to network fees for every crypto transference.

Start Using the Purchased Crypto

Investors need to transfer their money from a crypto wallet to a crypto bank. The banks connect an individual to debtors who pay interest to use their money for investments or grasps. Most debtors use the capital for margin trading, and few use the capital for fiat currency purchases. Some traders fancy using borrowing capital instead of vending their crypto to minimize capital profits. Others might have bullish insights on the crypto holdings and decide not to sell them. Crypto banks are different when it comes to the variety of cryptocurrencies accessible and easy platform usage.

Tip: One can use Compound and Celsius. The Compound can be used efficiently, and its DApp is accessible in the Coinbase Wallet. The trader can observe their capital growth and take the capital whenever they want to; liquid platform. Moreover, it gives individuals plenty of cryptocurrencies with huge interests. Celsius reimburses interest weekly hence not liquid as Compound, but its interests are more outstanding than Compound's.

The cryptocurrency industry is incredibly upsurging. It started with Bitcoin rather than Ethereum, and all altcoins are seemingly heading in the same direction. Therefore, individuals interested in cryptocurrency and who would like to invest should gain adequate knowledge before risking their money. Besides, they should avoid social media rumors and research using authorized material such as published books and journals.

Chapter 6 - Securing Your Assets

Everybody has security concerns when investing in a new field, such as in Decentralized Finances. DeFi's primary concern is the smart contract threat. Most companies believe that the fear of fraud is preventing most firms from adopting the Decentralized Finances concept.

The concerns show that there are honest security concerns that DeFi can bring to a firm. Utilization of bugs in codes and manipulating external value feed for stocks are the most recognized attack approaches.

For example, in 2020, two attacks occurred; one permitted the oracle value of insurance to be altered. The other involved theft of assets worth around $70 million USD from smart contracts. The incident raised some critics and motivated people to research more about DeFi to adopt it effectively. The following concepts offer guidelines on how one can give more security to their assets.

Talking About Security

Security Issues People have when investing

Vulnerable Wallets

Most Cryptocurrencies have genuine vulnerability when hacking attacks and robbery are concerned. Edinburgh University conducted research and reported that Hardware folders had several weaknesses that hackers could exploit. The researchers used malware to interrupt communication between the folders and the computers. The safety breach impacts cryptocurrencies users since their money can be diverted to other accounts easily.

Double Spending

The cryptocurrency industry is becoming more robust against planned double-spends. However, some individuals can compose attacks that allow them to use one coin twice in the same deal. For instance, person A can buy goods from the person and pay them using X BTC.

Person A proceeds to perform a similar deal to an address he manages using the same BTC. Person B might trust person A and fail to confirm; the BTC may be credited to person A's address, and person B gets nothing. Person B cannot make the transaction invalid since the BTC are not reversible. Besides, recourse is not possible since Bitcoin is uncontrolled.

Selfish Mining

Some Cryptocurrencies mining pools are strong enough to demand specific mining ratios. The collections might engage in selfish mining due to the power they possess. For example, such pools can mine a block and hide it from other genuine miners. The collections then look for a second block, and if they find it, they are ahead of other miners and end up receiving all rewards. Moreover, greedy miners can use Sybil attacks to invalidate deals on the system.

Over 50 Percent Attacks

A pool powerful enough can demand over fifty percent of the mining strength. This poses a danger to the Cryptocurrencies network. A collection with such force can manipulate deals by mining unacceptable blocks and double-spending. ASICS mining rigs ensure that most excavators can only do it in pools. However, some pools give much strength to the point of them being misused.

The security concerns can be remedied to reduce challenges facing the Crypto world. Everyone who has invested or looking forward to investing in Crypto should know the issues and how they can impact their investments.

The Power of Smart Contracts

It is a program that manages digital assets. Smart Contracts function in partnership with Blockchain technology. It uses computer software that mechanically performs specifications written into the program code. The code consists of agreement conditions between buyers and sellers, and it is self-performed depending on the preset occasions. The most renowned smart contract platform is Ethereum.

How Smart Contracts Produce Codes that Support DeFi Transactions

Smart contract safety functions via similar notions as those of any program. Codes that support DeFi deals have to be written, tested, and insured.

- Writing- Smart contract codes are generated by quality programming practices. The exercise reduces the possibility of attackers accessing the codes. A firm using smart contracts should ensure that the codes used are quality. The firms can get information on how to generate secure codes from various websites. For example, Ethereum has published instructions guiding individuals or firms on how to create smart contracts securely.

- Testing- Testing codes is another puzzle. Examining codes enhances the safety of the available software. The runtime performance is tested. A firm can do this independently or can opt to seek help from expert companies such as Certik.

- Insuring- People are well conversant with insurance in health, work, and automobiles. As individuals and companies continue using smart contracts, smart contract failure insurances become more significant, particularly to well-established companies. The insurance takes care of any financial hack in a company.

Role of Smart Contracts in System Security and Transactions

Smart contracts play significant roles in various industries as far as security issues are concerned.

1) Government Voting System

Smart contracts give a safe environment that makes the polling network less vulnerable to manipulation. Balloting using intelligent contracts is ledger-secured hence tricky for anyone to decode. Besides, this type of voting raises the number of voters since there is no need to queue, identify, and submit documents.

2) Healthcare

Blockchain keeps the programmed healthiness registers of patients with a secret key. Only the permitted persons can access the registers. Moreover, studies can be carried out secretly and safely using smart contracts. Hospital receipts can be stored in smart contracts and mechanically shared with indemnification firms as evidence of amenity. The register is also used for varying events like supply management, drug supervision, and compliance directive.

3) Supply Chain

The Supply chain industry has been suffering because of manually-based systems. Documents need to go via several channels before they are accepted. The whole procedure raises the dangers of scams and losses. Blockchain nullifies such stakes by bringing an available and safe, modern form to individuals participating in the chain. Besides, smart agreements are applied in stock administration and mechanization of payouts and jobs.

4) Financial Services

Blockchain aids in converting conventional monetary services in many means. In insurance petitions, smart contracts check faults, paths, and transference payouts to users if everything is correct. They integrate crucial equipment for accounting and get rid of potential penetration of accounting registers. Stakeholders are also allowed to make decisions in an apparent method. Moreover, smart contracts are applied in trade clearance; money is moved after calculating all the trade disbursement totals.

Benefits of Smart Contracts:

- Transparency- The information on the blockchain is accessible by every interested individual.

- Efficiency- Smart agreements do not give a chance for misunderstanding or loss of documents. "Code is law" is an expression used to expound the conduct.

- Cost Reduction- Smart contracts eradicate intermediaries in trades. The eradication significantly decreases the cost involved in the procedures.

- Security- Cryptography enhances the safety of deals and also prevents attacks such as double-spending from occurring.

Should you be Scared of Hacks and Exploits?

Limitation of Smart Contracts

Hard to Change

Altering the procedures of the intelligent contract is nearly unmanageable. Correction of a fault in a code consumes plenty of time, and the process is costly.

Loopholes Possibility

Denoting the notion of good faith, participants will transact fairly. The participants will not acquire funds unethically from the agreement. However, smart contract usage makes it hard to guarantee that the conditions of the treaty are met.

Third-Party

Smart contracts try to get rid of intermediaries in transactions, but it is impossible to do so. The third-party performs diverse duties from the ones they serve in traditional agreements. For instance, in smart contracts, attorneys will not be required when preparing individual agreements. However, lawyers are required by developers to comprehend the terms to generate codes for the smart contracts.

Vague Terms

Most contracts contain conditions that the participants do not fully comprehend. Smart agreements cannot handle vague conditions all the time.

How Hacks and Exploits are Possible

The up-surging economic landscape in the Crypto market has attracted fraudsters and hackers. Primarily unaudited smart contracts combined with duplicated codes have been a recipe for weaknesses and exploitations. This results in the theft of digital stocks worth many millions of dollars. In November 2020, all DeFi frauds added to fifty percent, according to the Cipher Trace Report. It was reported that there was a possible regulatory crackdown since regulators didn't have a compliance agreement against money laundering. 2021 will possibly bring more clarity on what procedures should be undertaken to avoid the effects of not complying with AML, sanctions, and Capture the Flag.

Example

bZx was the most attacked platform in the year 2020. Three attacks were conducted, and two of them were consecutive. The two attacks utilized the interconnection of the Decentralized Finances contracts and got away with approximately 900,000 USD. By obtaining huge flash loans than those they could get in normal circumstances, the attackers could influence stock prices and drain the lending group.

DAO Hack and Parity Hack

• DAO Hack

DAO stands for Decentralized Autonomous Organization. Programmers were focused on solving specific issues when a hacker commenced exploiting this opportunity to get Ether from DAO tokens. On June eighteenth, the hacker succeeded to transfer approximately 3.6m Ether into a fake DAO. This led to the price of Ether falling to under 13 USD. Individuals tried to divide DAO to inhibit more Ether from being drained, but they could accumulate adequate votes within a short period. Unfortunately, all Ether was placed in a lone address, and the invader only ceased after learning about the fork proposal. People could not access Ether from the fake DAO for a month. The fake DAO had the same configuration, flaws, and weaknesses as the real DAO. The hacker might have placed a short position before performing the hack, and he possibly got his returns when the Ether worth was reduced by half. The Ethereum Foundation could invalidate Ether in the fake DAO, and this complicates issues more.

• Parity Hack

Devops199 utilized a weakness within the smart contract library code. The hack led to the blockage of approximately 500 wallets holding a sum of roughly 500,000 Ether and other tokens. Wallet Library was established in July after the initial Parity Hack. Besides, an individual should take note of "only-uninitialized" and "destroy" lines. In November, a special deal was sent to Wallet Library using the initiWallet way. The deal made a particular address to the solitary owner, and after half an hour, Devops199 generated Parity matter to register what had recently happened. Parity realized the problem hours later and held all money in multi-sig folders positioned after July twentieth.

Approaches to Recover the Funds

• **Hardfork**

Recovery of funds can be made together with the arranged Constantinople hardfork. Hardforking Ethereum is followed by consequences ranging from social, political, and philosophical; it can result in "Ethereum Classic."

• **Implementing EIP156**

It gives a communal-managed way to retrieve funds during such occurrences. EIP doesn't necessarily provide a solution for the issue, but it indicates that there is potential that the community can adopt this technique to avoid a hardfork.

The Greedy, the Prodigal, and the Suicidal

a) Greedy

The contracts remain active and padlock Ether indefinitely. This permits Ether to be released as "greedy" under no terms. A good example is the Parity attack occurrence. The many sig-folder-like agreements which held Ether released money to users using the Parity Library agreement functions. The Parity Library was closed; hence the wallet agreements couldn't access it, leading to "greed." The situation resulted in padlocking of Ether worthy of approximately 200M USD. Greedy contracts can also result from simple faults. This happens to agreements that accept Ether, but either wholly lacks guidelines to send Ether out or cannot access such policies.

b) Prodigal

Such agreements always return the money when under attack. The funds are sent to addresses with a particular solution; bounties or those that have sent Ether in the past; lotteries. However, a vulnerability occurs when the contract sends Ether to a wrong address, one that has never deposited Ether in the agreement or to an arbitrary address.

c) Suicidal

Such agreement allows a safety fallback alternative of its owner killing it when it malfunctions or when attacked. The possibility of any arbitrary address killing the contract exposes a significant vulnerability hence termed as "suicidal" A good example is the Parity Fiasco incident. A random account killed a library agreement were the important Parity agreement relied upon. The parity was regarded as non-functional, and all the Ether was locked.

How one can Use the Knowledge when Venturing into DeFi

Symbolic Analysis

The concept takes agreement bytecode and examines particulars as inputs. The specifications include weaknesses class to look for and the innovation depth. The symbolic analysis element is established by the implantation of a primary Ethereum Virtual Machine. The machine carries out symbolic execution of the agreement bytecode. The feature operates potential performance traces symbolically till it locates a trail that satisfies certain preset aspects. The inputs in each performance trace involve several symbolic variables. The eventual step consists of running the agreement concretely and validating the answers for genuine positives. The concrete Validation element performs this function.

Concrete Validation

The element takes results created by symbolic analysis and examines the agreement's exploit on a confidential form of Ether blockchain. It is an examination bed used to confirm the accuracy of the bugs. After the test, the agreement is regarded as true or false. The agreement on the primary blockchain is not impacted since no alterations are done to the official Ether blockchain.

Three Ways to Secure Smart Contracts

Using Particular Blockchain Development Exercises

Smart contracts require development exercises that consider the particulars of blockchain technology. Mihail says that the value of development error in a smart contract is higher than in other program solutions. One should take their time when writing the codes to avoid making critical faults that can be avoided. For instance, the mechanisms of many blockchain systems permit one to call the code of agreement unexpectedly. New developers might ignore the problem and write invalid codes.

Being Careful about Excess Functionality

Smart contracts have great functionality, which makes platforms such as EOS and Ethereum renown. The functionality sometimes results in security issues, as the blockchain expert; Mihail indicates. When one is functioning with procedures that support complicated smart contracts, one should follow the appropriate exercise of the corresponding smart contracts system. Some systems such as Ziliqa and Cardano aid programmers in improving their codes' security by putting additional restrictions on the blockchain. The systems allow programmers to generate authentication tools contracts that give them a hundred percent assurance of their smart contracts security.

Selecting the Programming Language Sensibly

The language selected while writing smart contract codes should be secured. Languages such as C++ and JavaScript offer programmers a variety of chances to develop complicated, highly operational agreements.

Most blockchains create their encoding language to decrease possible bugs and faults in a code. One should be aware of many aspects, including integration between the language, the compiler, and the smart contract. Scilla is an example of less complicated languages; it is used to write Ziliqa blockchains. The simple languages enable the programmers to write codes without making mistakes. One should always follow the best exercises as per the inventor of the languages and the blockchain involved.

The adoption of smart contracts continues to increase every day. The increase is because smart contracts use information feeds, which can be anything; Virustotal API or demographic calculation of America. In hypothesis, a capitalization manager specializes in the number of new viruses likely to emerge the following day. People can then invest in their ideal manager. Smart contracts have disadvantages like any other fresh technology. Therefore, smart contracts can be safer if developers have adequate knowledge of the field.

Section 3: Familiarizing the Popular Defi Use Cases

Chapter 7 – Learn About Decentralized Exchange

Decentralized exchanges are the third-largest class of DeFi products. They work in a similar way as a stock exchange except instead of having a central provider, DEXs' exchange is via smart contracts found in blockchains such as Ethereum. Rules on how the transaction is to go are predetermined in the smart contract code. That way users always interact with the contract so as to trade their assets.

Unlike cryptocurrency exchanges, decentralized exchanges (DEXs) do not have the sign-up process hassles like putting in your email, coming up with a strong password, and account verification. In decentralized exchanges, trading happens directly between wallets with minimal input from any intermediaries.

DeFining What It Is

A decentralized exchange is what's most fascinating about the DeFi revolution. DEX is a peer-to-peer exchange that connects buyers and sellers directly instead of them transacting within a centralized exchange. More coins are listed in a DEX than a centralized exchange.

DEXs work in a manner that money is collected through smart contracts and routed relative to the best price using an oracle.

No DEX has the ability to trade between fiat currency and crypto because in fiat currency there needs to be a third party recording the account balance.

How Is Different from a Centralized Exchange?

There are various items that one somebody cannot purchase using Bitcoin yet and for one to acquire most cryptocurrencies, you have to first exchange them for a fiat currency. So, the only solution to exchange coins without any third-party involvement is decentralized exchanges.

In centralized exchanges, the systems are kept off-chain. This is to show that they act as escrows for the individuals transacting there and no records are kept on the blockchain. Such transactions are not safe and private keys can be easily assessed by hackers.

On the other hand, decentralized exchanges enable peer-to-peer transactions to take place. Traders are therefore custodians of their own money.

WHAT MAKES DEXs ADVANTAGEOUS.

Transaction fees are cheaper.

Compared to centralized exchanges, trading on DEXs is much cheaper. Traders are always looking for the lowest rates in the market whenever they want to trade assets they own. An example is Uniswap which only charges a 0.3% trading fee. The only way centralized exchanges will be able to compete with DEXs is if they lowered their fees.

Privacy.

Privacy on your activities in the crypto market is really important. DEXs promote that since there are no registration requirements to use DEXs and so there is a reduced risk of someone collecting any kind of data about you. Decentralized exchanges only use addresses in transactions.

Financial Inclusiveness.

DEXs allow anyone from any part of the world to use them. Centralized exchanges however restrict individuals from some jurisdictions from using their services. DEXs are therefore much more inclusive.

Lower counterparty risk.

Over the years, we are always hearing stories that billions of dollars have been stolen by hackers in the centralized exchange. Such an issue is foreign in decentralized exchanges. Smart contracts make it impossible for fraudsters and scammers to steal. This is because certain conditions are set by the traders during an exchange and the conditions have to be dutifully followed for the whole operation to go through.

In addition to that, decentralized exchanges only work through a certain network of computers that are only interconnected with each other.

Robustness.

DEXs are quite solid since they do not operate using just a single server like it is done in centralized exchanges. There's a very minimal chance for a DEX system to crash.

THE INNER WORKINGS OF DEXs

Decentralized exchanges work in the same manner as peer-to-peer platforms. Users have total control over the assets they are trading without involving any intermediaries.

Instant loans are available to users on the DEX platforms with the aid of their assets as collateral.

In the DEXs where users pool their digital assets in the liquidity pools, the users get returns in form of either complimentary tokens or even in the form of interest. Decentralized exchanges solely work with the aid of smart contracts. The smart contracts are publicly described between the parties trading so they can give each other precise conditions.

Some DEXs such as Aave make it possible for users to earn interest when they make deposits and when they borrow assets too. The decentralized applications (dApps) in DeFi trade on the DEXs. These are entirely peer-to-peer. The decentralized applications are open source and permissionless public blockchains developed in the DeFi ecosystem.

Decentralized exchanges have order books that may exist either on-chain or off-chain. In on-chain, they're hosted on a distributed ledger, and on off-chain, they're hosted by third parties.

On-chain order books

On-chain order books are directly hosted on the distributed ledger. Note that all orders are usually submitted to the distributed ledger network and then confirmed by the network. Users have the ability to host and access the order book and any individual can freely submit personal orders to be included in the order book. All of that is possible for as long as the distributed ledger is made public.

Bitshares and Stellar decentralized exchanges are great examples of on-chain order books. After users submit their orders in the Stellar network, the orders are then hosted on a public on-chain order book in the network's distributed ledger. All information in the orders is then broadcast to all the Stellar validator nodes and is made possible for the public to view.

Trade is automatically executed and settled by the Stellar network as soon as two orders intersect in price.

On-chain order books are really difficult to manipulate and thus impossible for anyone to make private details. Orders are specifically published on a specific node.

On-chain order books are extremely easy to use since one does not need to deposit funds to trade but you can instead buy tokens directly to your wallet. On-chain order books are not expensive and selling tokens on them is so efficient.

Off-chain order books

Off-chain order books on the other hand are hosted by an intermediary outside of the distributed ledger. The third-party host is a centralized entity that helps involved users discover the other users that make offers on assets and restrict access to either view or submit the order book.

Off-chain transactions can be made possible through multiple methods including:

- Users can have a transfer agreement between themselves.

- An intermediary can be involved in the transactions so as to ensure no one has ripped off their assets.

- The other way for off-chain transactions to be executed is via using a coupon-based payment method. An individual will buy coupons in exchange for crypto tokens. The individual then gives the code to the other party to redeem them either in the same transacting cryptocurrency or even a different one. Well, that's totally dependent on the coupon service provider.

Automated market makers.

In the financial market, Automated Market Makers (AMMs) help keep the DeFi ecosystem liquid all day, every day using liquidity pools. In short, AMMs are part of the DeFi ecosystem and they allow permissionless and automatic trading of assets via the liquidity pools rather than the traditional market we are used to of buyers and sellers.

AMMs are unique to DeFi and Ethereum and are always available for trading. This exchange method allows anyone to participate and if they feel like building new solutions there is no one to hold them back.

The DeFi ecosystem has three AMM models that are quite dominant. They are:

● Uniswap; which allows traders to create a liquidity pool with any pair of ERC-20 tokens.

● Balancer allows its users to create liquidity pools of up to eight assets in a ratio that are quite dynamic.

● Curve creates liquidity pools of similar assets for example stablecoins. Curve solves the limited liquidity problem while offering the cheapest and most efficient trades in the market.

LIMITATIONS OF DEXs

Liquidity.

Decentralized exchanges are still new in the market and they support a wide range of trading pairs. Market segregation that's currently in place has a negative impact on the liquidity the market has. Asset liquidity has also been increasing with the growth of DeFi.

Poor user experience.

It is quite challenging for users who are not familiar with the operation of DEXs to navigate through the blockchain. The first thing users are supposed to get familiar with is the external wallets in order to interact with a DEX. After that users are required to fund their wallets via transferring crypto or any fiat currency. They should then link the funded wallet to the DEX interface in order to execute a trade. Such a long process can be quite confusing for new traders since it is not straightforward.

Scalability.

When it comes to blockchain scalability, it totally depends on the transactions a network can process before attaining capacity. An example is Bitcoin and Ethereum. Bitcoin's network processes 4.6 transactions per second, while Ethereum's is at 15 transactions per second. DEXs work using smart contracts which live on blockchain networks. DEXs are therefore bound by the limits of the network's infrastructure.

On and Off-Ramps.

The current decentralized exchange technology doesn't support the buying of digital assets with fiat currency. The technology still does not allow a person to trade the fiat or even withdraw anything into your bank account. Such limitations in the DeFi ecosystem act as barriers to entry for beginner users.

DEX TOP APPLICATIONS

Most of the people in the blockchain scene believe that DEXs are the future of crypto trading. This is because traders face a lot of challenges when using centralized exchanges. In order for someone to start trading using centralized exchanges to have to first buy assets through some fiat gateway services which have really high transaction fees.

The exchanges have to then hold private keys to your tokens and coins for you. That is called a custodial exchange. The custodial system forces exchanges to manage wallets that oftentimes contain too much wealth. This is definitely targeted by hackers who over the years have always managed to steal so much since the centralized exchange is not as secure.

The solution to all these problems traders face with their assets is decentralization where there are no third parties needed to hold funds or anything when individuals are trading assets. In addition, decentralized exchanges provide better transparency and they can consent to unlimited trading pairs using technology. Some of the best decentralized exchanges include:

Ox Protocol – ERC-20 DEX

Ox is a hybrid DEX model that tells a user what the smart contracts deployed on the Ethereum blockchain know and how to carry out a trade using them. Ox depends on a relayer model since on-chain order books are slow and expensive. The relayer in Ox, lexicon, refers to a method that hosts order books in a centralized database. Lexicon also matches orders between two trades. Some examples of relayers are ERC dEX, DDEX, Radar Relay, and Paradex.

Let us use an example so as to get how the Ox architecture functions.

Brian creates an order using DDEX, which then goes to the centralized database. DDEX can share this with other relayers so that more users can see the order.

Esther wants to accept Brian's order and so she executes the order using DDEX. DDEX will automatically match the request and send it to an Ox smart contract to complete the order.

When executing the orders, Brian and Esther let smart contracts to cut the fees from their wallets. The Ox smart contracts will then verify the order and put a completion to the token transfer on-chain. The ZRX token is what's used in Ox to pay the transaction fees.

The biggest benefit Ox has is that various DEXs and relayers can co-exist while sharing the same liquidity pool and the same protocol. Ox is not compatible with the Bitcoin protocol but instead only works with Ether and ERC tokens.

IDEX – ERC-20 DEX.

IDEX also just supports tokens from the Ethereum ecosystem.

IDEX functions in this manner. You deposit funds and smart contracts are the ones that control the funds. The Ethereum blockchain functions as the settlement layer in IDEX though all transactions have to be first updated on a centralized database before they're written into the blockchain.

IDEX has very high liquidity and it has a utility token called IDEX which secures the network on which IDEX runs.

IDEX enforces user registration in 2019. This is a counterparty risk which then raises questions about the platform's future.

Waves DEX

Waves has its own blockchain and its own token (WAVES) which is an important part of the DEX platform.

Trading fees are first paid in the WAVES token. There's the option of creating your own token via paying 1 WAVES, which gets listed on the Waves DEX automatically.

Although Waves DEX is centralized in various respects, it is still a non-custodial exchange. Trades are not peer-to-peer as the order books are centralized. The trades are made through an intermediary therefore not on-chain. The intermediary then makes the transactions on-chain before completing the swap between the two traders.

Nash Exchange

This decentralized exchange supports Bitcoin. It has off-chain order matching and trade settlements which are made via smart contracts. The off-chain order matching engine is a distributed engine that is designed to initially run with five nodes.

To carry out trades in Nash Exchange, traders should first lock their money in a smart contract. The off-chain order matching engine then relays data between the smart contracts and the blockchain's peer-to-peer network. As soon as the order is matched, traders should sign off on the transaction before the trade is settled. The money is then exchanged and immediately put back into the trader's wallet. The Nash Exchange requires traders to register and that is definitely not an indication of decentralization.

Loopring – Layer 2 Scaling Protocol for Ethereum.

Loopring is a modular protocol that builds DEXs on various blockchains.

You can use a wallet interface such as Metamask to create orders and then sign them with your own private key. This action allows Loopring to withdraw funds when the trade is being executed. As long as the order is not matched, the trader has full control of funds even after they have placed an order.

Loopring can match 16 trades times since it enables the UniDirectional Order Method. When all orders get matched by ring-miners, they are then signed off and sent back to the Loopring protocol to settle the transaction. The smart contracts in the protocol settle all trades on-chain.

Loopring is currently only limited to Ethereum. It can also be implemented on other public blockchains but that's possible via support from smart contracts.

Kyber Protocol – ERC-20 DEX

This is a set of smart contracts which provide a decentralized manner to perform on-chain swaps. In this protocol, a reserve is what someone who provides liquidity is called. The reserve is responsible for providing liquidity to traders and they can also provide registration to Kyber's smart contracts.

Let's use an example so as to get how the Kyber protocol works. If you want to purchase DAI tokens in place of 1 Ether, the Kyber smart contracts asks various reserves for the best exchange price. If you want to proceed with the exchange after you've learnt about the exchange rate, you send 1 Ether to a smart contract in the Kyber network. The reserve then does an on-chain exchange and your account is credited with the DAI tokens.

The Kyber protocol is only limited to Ethereum and ERC tokens. There's hope for it to enable trading for different blockchains in the coming future.

Chapter 8: Adding a Bit of Complexity

The blockchain industry is the most promising innovation occurring in the monetary world today. The decentralized finance generated an economic upheaval and a significant impact on the forthcoming generations. The DeFi universe has overcome the current crisis, the Covid pandemic, by breaking records sequentially.

The records have shown that DeFi is a conducive environment to conduct business every year. The DeFi universe achieves highs for the sum of value locked, swapping volumes, involvement, and everyday active users. The outstanding metrics and rapid growth of DeFi gives us an insight into what its future will be like. Moreover, derivatives have great potential and are very significant to the DeFi world. Why is this the case?

Meet the Decentralized Derivative

The decentralized derivative is monetary security. Derivative's worth is retrieved from underlying assets, indexes, interest rates, or assets. It is a contract between two individuals or more, and the assets are generally bought through brokerages. Moreover, derivatives are swapped either over the counter or through an exchange. The over the counter (OTC)) trades are riskier since they involve two confidential parties who are unregulated. The counterparty risk, the possibility that one party may default the terms of the transactions, is what either party faces. Primarily, derivatives were meant for ensuring that products swapped worldwide had a flat rate of exchange. Currently, derivatives rely on several deals, and they have a variety of uses. For instance, some derivatives rely on weather information like the number of sunny days in an area.

Derivatives have various uses such as:

- Hedging a position

- Speculating the direction an underlying stock is likely to move

- Giving leverage to holdings.

Pros

The accessibility-An individual is only needed to have an Ethereum wallet and connectivity to the internet.

Surpassing Barriers- The decentralized derivatives can overcome challenges of any kind; geographical, social, and monetary.

Affordability-Generating a primary derivative is cheap and can be performed by any individual who knows the basics about blockchain technology.

Democratic and confidentiality- The deals regarding derivatives are conducted in a fair and efficient market. Besides, the privacy of the parties involved in a particular transaction is upheld.

Flexibility- The derivatives deals are flexible enough such that an individual can perform them anywhere anytime as long as they have an internet connection.

Cons

Network Charges- The internet used to carry derivatives deals is not freely offered, and one needs to pay for it.

Delayed deals- Most of the derivatives' deals are done through the internet, and sometimes the internet is overcrowded. The overcrowding causes delays in transactions which can be frustrating.

Corruption- Since anybody with blockchain knowledge can perform derivative deals with no legalization, funds can be stolen. The money can be circulated on the platform leading to corruption.

Bugs- The smart contracts sometimes have faults that can affect the derivatives deals.

How Does This Even Work?

The Process

Derivatives are monetary instruments that are worthless on their own. Therefore, derivatives retrieve their value from other instruments such as indices and assets. Derivatives rely wholly on other monetary instruments, and they have their purpose. They are used in circumstances where they are required to reduce the business charges for a deal. In other moments, they are used to generate returns. Some traders engage in derivatives because they have to, while others do so out of willingness.

The risks associated with derivatives can be managed easily through hedging. The risks include value, expiration, and counterparty dangers. Hedging is performed when the danger of a particular asset is transmitted from one trader to another. Derivatives are used for speculation by traders who want to get profits. An investor can exploit the increase of the price of the stock that underlies the derivatives. Traders who take advantage can reap huge gains.

Kinds of Derivatives

For investors to efficiently use derivatives, they need to understand their types. There are two major kinds which include Exchange Traded and Over Counter Derivatives. There are other three sections based on the two significant kinds; swaps, alternatives, and futures.

Futures - They are monetary instruments that enable an individual to purchase an asset at a forthcoming date using the present value on the marketplace. Forward and futures agreements are examples of OTDs and ETDs, respectively.

Options - They are agreements that permit a trader to purchase or retail an asset without suggesting a responsibility to retail and purchase. The value of closing this deal is fixed, and it is termed as "strike value."

Swaps - The agreement permits investors to trade the underlying worth of commodities, shares, bonds, and coinages before a particular forthcoming date.

Investors can decide to use CFDs (Contract for Difference) on bonds, indices, and commodities. Individuals engaging in indices swapping use value movements of indices to generate returns. The traders must use CFDs as support when swapping indices since they lack the physical foundation to be swapped alone. Contract for Difference is an agreement between a trader and a capitalization bank. It involves the interchange of the variance between the concluding and initial value of particular monetary instruments.

The CFD swapping of commodities is applied in economic marketplace speculations. The commodities are swapped in two ways which include forward and cash. The Share CFDs enable investors to have accessibility to a stock marketplace of multiple firms. Individuals' swaps depend on the firm's share price movements. The firms have to be those that trade in the equity marketplace. Besides, investors are not required to be the owner of the underlying asset, which is an added advantage of swapping CFDs. The latter relieves investors from worries of bankruptcy and disastrous occurrences.

Heard of These Synthetic Assets?

What are Synthetic Projects?

Synthetic projects are monetary instruments that accelerate other instruments. Synthetics consist of either a single or more derivatives that rely on the worth of an underlying stock. Examples of such stocks include forward commitments, futures and forwards, contingent claims, swaps, alternatives, and credit derivatives. Investors decided to purchase synthetic assets because of their funding, liquidity generation, and market accessibility.

How Synthetic Projects are done under Decentralized Derivatives

The synthetic projects are formed similarly. Two parties are formulated where one is short and the other long. After a short period, the network transmits collateral from one side to another depending on value movement. The transference is also determined by the configuration of the mechanized agreement arbitrating between the sides. The synthetic projects are over-collateralized to avoid trust requirements between the participants. The projects are managed directly by smart agreement networks.

Synthetix

It is a network that permits investors to mint fresh crypto stocks. The fresh stocks imitate both the reality universe; USD and crypto stocks; BTC. The services are facilitated by the use of codes alone and don't require monetary mediators. Synthetix is a set of smart contracts operating on Ether blockchain. The fresh stocks are created through the collateralization procedure. Collateralization involves investors purchasing SNX crypto, storing it in specific contracts, and later using them to create the Synths. Synths trail the worth of other stocks using oracles; specific information feeds.

mStable

It is a platform for individuals to mint mUSD; customizable stable stock. The platform to perform no-slip stablecoin trades and produce income. The mUSD provides high worth stability, passive income, and a shield from perpetual investment loss. It is minted from a tokenized collection of base stablecoin stocks. The base stocks include; USDC and TUSD. mUSD has several advantages such as recollateralization mechanisms, less centralization, and communal management.

Mirror

It is a procedure that governors manage. Mirror coin has to be risked to vote on live ballots, and it acts as the deposit of producing fresh governance polls. In the coming days, MIR will serve more aims that raise its utility and worth.

The decentralized derivatives are growing at a rapid rate. It is crucial to watch other developing projects, such as Vega, UMA, and CloseCross. The data indicates that the full potential of derivatives may explode this year.

Five Derivatives Indexes You Should Know

What are Indices?

Indices are a dimension of the value performance of a set of bonds from an interchange. For instance, the FTSE 100 trails the 100 biggest firms on the London asset exchange. Swapping indices permits traders to have exposure to a whole sector at once by opening one position. CFDs aid investors in predicting the value movements of indices without owning the underlying asset. Moreover, indices are highly volatile and have more extended trading periods than other marketplaces. The longer periods expose traders to multiple chances of making profits. One can commence swapping indices by using an IG account.

How Indices helps Traders DeFi Investment Journey

1) Going Long or Short

When an investor is swapping indices using CFDs, they can be lengthy or petite. Going lengthy indicates that the investor is purchasing the marketplace because they speculate that the value will increase. On the other hand, going petite indicates that the investor is retailing the marketplace because they predict that the value will drop. Gains or losses are determined by the investor's speculation accuracy and the available size of the marketplace movement.

2) Swapping with Leverage

CFDs are leveraged commodities. This indicates that an investor is only required to devote a bit of initial pledge; margin to open points provides them with enormous marketplace exposure. Traders swapping with leverage should know that their gains or losses are measures using the whole point size. The returns or losses aren't only determined by the primary margin used for opening it.

3) Hedging the Existing Positions

A trader with a set of varying bonds may short indices. This is mainly to offer self-protection from losses to the trader's portfolio. If the marketplace starts going downwards and their bonds commence losing worth, the sharp point on the indices will rise in worth. This balances the losses from the assets. However, if the assets' worth increases, the short indices points would only take a part of the trader's returns. Moreover, a trader who has opened short positions on several assets that feature on indices can enter a long position to hedge against stakes. If the indices increase in value, their position will get returns, neutralizing losses on the trader's short asset positions.

Different DeFi Derivatives Projects that are Currently Up

Compound: COMP

An investor can deposit and gain interest or borrow against the COMP. One can also offer liquidity to a collection of COMP symbols and gain interest. The interest rate is measured according to the request and supply of the symbols. The owners of Compound symbols are allowed to vote either supporting or opposing the COMP protocol.

Pros

- Standardizes Bitcoin and altcoins

- It can be used in DApps

- Multiple supplies of coins

Cons

- The safety of the stored assets is worrisome.

Synthetix: SNX

The SNX symbols, when staked by the owners, get minted into Synthetic stocks. The platform used is called MIntr. The platform permits traders to stake against Eth. Individuals staking their SNX symbol for minting the synthetic stocks earn 0.30 % of the swap's worth. The inflationary regulation implementation led to the sudden upsurge of the Synthetix symbol.

Pros

- No intermediaries required in transactions

- Comfortability and assurance when trading the tokens

- Exposure to the real world in a short period

Cons

- Interdependence on the Ether Synthetix network

- Regulatory policies

Chainlink: LINK

The LINK token possesses the most significant marketplace cap. The Chainlink allows traders to obtain information, disbursements, and other occurrences without risking their assets. It has an oracle that offers external information to provoke the performance of the smart contracts. Besides, it provides traders with approximately four percent interest rates.

Pros

- Trustless bridge between blockchains

- It can be used with any blockchain

- First mover in the decentralized oracle

Cons

- Above a half, od supply is managed by the primary firm

- Its oracle system is still limited

Uniswap Token: UNI

One of the most renowned DeFi tokens in the world. It offers approximately seven percent profits annually on the capital a trader keeps. UNI doesn't charge any rates for withdrawal and deposition of money. Besides, it gives high security, and the funds are not stored in hot wallets at all. Any individual who owns ETH can swap UNI, and this offers an added advantage.

Pros

- Easy accessibility to the crypto marketplace

- Generation of profits by just storing funds in the liquidity pool

- Available features such as fresh tokens

Cons

- The swap element depends on arbitrage swapping

- Fake tokens

Other tokens such as 1inch, Aave, Maker Dao, Universal Market Access, and Sushiswap. As time goes by, more tokens are being launched. The trend has the potential to continue in the future as more research continues to be conducted.

Get to Know These Four Options

What are the Options?

An option is an obligatory contract that permits a purchaser to retail or buys an underlying asset. The purchase is generally at a prearranged value, and it is within a specific period. The purchaser has the right but not a responsibility to buy or retail the underlying asset. What differentiates between alternative and futures agreements? In future agreements, one is obligated to handle the conveyance of the underlying asset.

For instance, there are charges linked with conveyance and stowage of the underlying, making the futures agreement to be valued negatively. Options Premium is the fee that a purchaser pays the alternative retailer to be granted the right to buy or retail a specific asset at a prearranged value.

Options Roles when Investing in Cryptocurrency

Protection

Holders- Alternatives guard theworth of investors who are holders. For instance, an investor who wants to purchase BTC for a long-term plan but isn't sure of how prices will be after a while can buy BTC and put alternatives to protect their assets.

Traders- Alternatives aids investors in practicing day swapping to guard their positions from possible losses. For example, if a trader wants to open a short position and purchases, Ethereum can call an alternative to guard their position.

Onboarding holders- Alternatives protect beginners in cryptocurrency investments. For instance, if a trader wants to purchase BTC for their relatives and doesn't want them to be discouraged if prices fall, they can purchase BTC and put alternatives to guard the assets. This will enable them to have peace of mind.

Hedging

One can hedge the worth of their future mining incomes using the alternatives. For example, If an investor knows how much Ethereum they will excavate next month and require funds to settle farm charges but are not assured of profits, they can hedge the Eth worth.

Examples of DeFi Derivatives Options Projects that Investors can look into and Explore

FinNexus- It is an open economic procedure constructed on the Wanchain blockchain. It is a pivot for linking various decentralized ledgers to one another and traders. Besides, it also links the traditional monetary applications.

Hegic- It is an on-chain alternative swapping protocol. It permits a trader to purchase Ethereum calls and put alternatives as to the sole holder. It also permits an investor to retail Ethereum calls and put alternatives as to the liquidity supplier.

Hetoro- It is a swapping and information examination platform for on-chain alternatives.

Lien- It is a procedure for generating alternatives and stablecoins from Ethereum.

Opyn- It is a smart contract that relies on an indemnity platform built on the Convexity Protocol. It gives a well-required and broad insurance resolution for the rapidly developing DeFi network.

The above examples are just a section of the multiple growing options and may change in the future. This is because the blockchain industry is rapidly growing, and more options will be generated as time goes by.

The notion of having an independent and decentralized derivatives marketplace is fascinating. However, the infrastructure to accomplish the goal is still inadequate in the underlying software. All resolutions available today are centralized and can easily manipulate information, either the interchange or elements used to publish the value. Smart contracts are a recommended idea that can transform technology by eliminating intermediaries. However, the notion of the underlying technology is at the concept level and not mature enough to be implemented in the real universe. Besides, there are still challenges for acquiring relevant cryptocurrencies to operate with.

Chapter 9 - Further Understanding Decentralized Insurance

The growth of the blockchain world is surging every day. The constant development of the DeFi has produced various cryptocurrency indemnity solutions. The solutions are designed for guarding against smart contracts agreement failures and other mechanical problems that can lead to significant losses in DeFi. Besides, the DeFi industry provides indemnity to individuals that require it most, hence resolving the real-life problem.

The industry is in an early stage and offers beginners an excellent opportunity to learn about the technology. There are various methods blockchain indemnity can be implemented, policies, projects, and the benefits that come along as discussed below:

What is Decentralized Insurance?

Meaning

Decentralized cover acquires various goals from the traditional cover marketplace. It safeguards individuals and organizations from monetary damage due to scams, theft, or unexpected infrastructure letdowns. The cover helps in safeguarding capitalizers and providers in case of attacks and other frauds. Developers such as Nexus Mutual and CDx offer DeFi cover resolutions. The solutions offer safety for everything ranging from deals on exchanges to loaning on Compound or Dharma.

Role in DeFi Transactions

Decentralized Exchanges- It involves P2P monetary deals where users manage their funds. DeFi cover protects the users of the exchange from theft, hacks, and other problems.

E-wallets- The wallets function independently and give traders accessibility to blockchain-formed plays. The DeFi cover ensures that the wallets are incurred against several risks, and so are the users.

Stable Coins-They try to steady their worth by linking the coins with non-crypto currencies such as USD. In the process, they are faced with various challenges, some of which can cause monetary damage. The cover ensures their losses are compensated, and this gives them more confidence.

Non-fungible Tokens- generate digital stocks from non-swappable stocks such as slam dunks videos, and the DeFi cover protects them during the procedures.

Pros

- Dependable and apparent services in contrast with traditional covers

- Efficient customer services

- It saves time since disbursements are mathematically confirmed and transacted within a short period.

- Easily accessible by participants since the fees charged are affordable.

- It accepts members from all over the world.

Cons

- Do not cover for everything that goes wrong in the DeFi procedure.

- Absence of secondary marketplace to swap. Traders swap in a public platform.

How does it Work?

DeFi cover targets shielding individuals from losses like the traditional economic universe. The shielded individuals pay a particular premium depending on the capital they are holding and the exchange they are using. The traditional cover policy is given and registered by a multinational consumer. However, the DeFi indemnity depends on the holders' community when charging premiums and arranging payments. If an individual undergoes a monetary loss, they can notify the indemnity and get remunerated immediately.

Some DeFi exchanges pay a certain premium for insurance against hacks. For example, if an exchange is hacked, the specific indemnity compensates all the individuals using that exchange. Furthermore, the DeFi cover can generate tokenized crypto stocks and also give valuable safeguard. The cover primarily engages in smart agreements, and the data is kept in a communal database. Users can take out indemnity policy on smart agreements, money, or other digital stocks. Nexus Mutual is the ideal example to help investors comprehend how Decentralized cover works and the procedure involved.

The Procedure:

• A smart agreement owner linked to a dApp that delivers amenities to consumers decided to safeguard its users. The protection is against monetary loss retrieved from using the dApp.

• The owner submits the smart contract to Nexus Mutual. The Nexus personnel create due diligence on the safety of the agreement, and if the confirmation provides favorable results, the agreement is added to the other coverable agreements.

• Investors who have understood the smart agreement, which is public in blockchain, decides to stake some amount in favor that the agreement won't default. The investors generate a "liquidity collection" by depositing a quantity of Nexus Mutual tokens. The "liquidity collection" is aimed at covering remuneration if a complaint covered by the policy occurs.

• Individuals willing to buy a risk indemnity pay the agreed premium. A portion of the premium is given to the stakers.

• The stakes income is connected to the number of policies bought on that specific agreement. The maximum period of staking and achievement of return equal to half of the deposited money is about 250 days.

• The stakers accommodates the danger that if the agreement causes losses to a single or more covered party, their staking amount is used to compensate the indemnities.

Different Crypto Insurance Policies

Digital Deposit Insurance

The indemnity involves the coverage for the DSPs; Digital Store-value Products. The monetary commodities permit customers to keep their funds in a digital setup. The funds can be topped up or withdrawn by the investor. The investor does various deposition functions regardless of the kind of entity providing the commodity. The deposition functions include payouts, liquidity, and money storage. Besides, accessibility of the commodities is through non-branch physical networks like agents, mobile phones, and modernized transactional podiums. In this case, the commodities include mobile funds, card-grounded electronic funds, and internet-grounded electronic funds. However, the products do not include mobile banking, Crypto coinages, and stowed-worth gift cards.

Approaches to Deposit Indemnity for DSPs

• Direct - A deposit coverer directly covers the DSPs, and their suppliers should have membership of the deposit indemnity network. Several nations like India and Mexico have embraced this approach. The nations have allowed banks to provide covered digital stored-value commodities. Besides, the nations have generated fresh specialized sets of controlled and monitored organizations to provide such commodities at low costs.

• Exclusion - In this method, DSPs are omitted from deposit indemnity coverage, and other means of shielding consumers are embracing. Peru and the Philippines are some of the nations that have embraced this approach. The countries being the decision-makers regard DSPs as general instruments of temporary worth stowage to make payouts or transferences.

• Pass-through -It is the most complicated and least adopted method. The deposit indemnity coverage "passes through" a private account to its member and holds consumers' money from DSPs. Some of the nations that have embraced this method include Kenya and Nigeria. In these countries, DSPs are offered by non-monetary institutions like technology and mobile operator firms.

Crypto-wallet Insurance

The policy was founded by Lloyd's. The policy was aimed at shielding cryptocurrency held in online folders against hacks and theft. It is a fresh kind of liability indemnity that either drops or rises as the value of crypto stocks changes. This indicates that the covered individual will be insured for the underlying worth of the stock even after it varies over the policy timeframe. The hot wallet launched by Lloyd's provides a pathway for constructing a market that gives better worth for consumers' fluctuating and diversified requirements. This is done through fast response and cutting-edge danger control in commodities and services.

Moreover, the insurance commodity was supported by the PIF member recently. Janczewski indicated that the insurance would help eliminate the theft and hack challenges and extend the demand for crypto. Other individuals gave recommendable remarks about the wallet coverage. For example, Maynard illustrated that the coverage gives a quick pathway to rise indemnity capacity for complicated and difficult-to-cover dangers.

Crypto-backed Collateralized Loan Insurance

The collateral shielding cover can lead to the mass embracement of token markets. The Consortium announcement was made in Switzerland, where a Decentralized Insurance Foundation had been generated. The foundation was aimed at controlling tokens created in the Token Sale. The establishment members include Etherisc and other firms that jointly have sets of crucial expertise. For example, bZx has established a devolved margin loaning procedure and an insolvency oracle market. The procedure has generated a loaning network that facilitates exposed accessibility to credit. Besides, the conglomerate includes Celsius Network, the founder of the P2P devolved borrowing and loaning platform. Moreover, Lendroid is part of the conglomerate, and it is a non-supervisory loaning podium for collateralized credits, advanced sale markets, and trust-autonomous margin swapping. ETHLend also gives P2P loaning smart agreement for loaning Ether.

Are credit counting procedures significant in the consortium? Colendi provides the credit counting procedure and a microcredit podium. Ripio Credit Network is generating a procedure that brings improved apparent and dependability in credit and loaning. The reverse of this notion is the prompt crypto-supported lends that originate from consortium member; Nexo.

Sweetbridge is the last establishing member of the consortium. It is a blockchain-founded monetary framework that transmutes supply chain logistics and aims at unleashing operational capital.

Payment Channel Insurance

The coverage aims to digitalize and expand the customer experience while upholding customer involvement and the quality of the general association with the institution. The PayTAS resolution suite has advanced into TAS InPAY that is compatible with the fresh needs in the digital indemnity. The advancement permits the industry to leverage a merged multiple-channel payout opening and reconciliation podium from TAS. The Inpay enables modernized satisfaction of the sales procedure for the indemnity industry. Furthermore, fulfillment permits the end-consumer to pay in a unified, real-moment means and select their favorite methods of payment and service. The TAS resolution can administer the entire credit position on behalf of the coverer and arrange lone payouts related to it. Moreover, it merges innovative pool approaches which unlock a truthfully mobile consumer experience. The consumer conforms to every local payout criteria and effortlessly adapts to any possible fresh payout schemes emerging from the marketplace.

Three DeFi Projects that Covers Insurance

What they are and the insurance policies they offer

Nexus Mutual

The project is generating decentralized indemnity on Ether by using a danger-sharing collection. Its members manage the pool, and the Nexus Mutual tokens indicate their rights. The NXM is primarily established with smart agreement indemnity allowing everyone to buy insurance on any community ETH smart agreement. The step indicates that DeFi users can acquire shields on their money being loaned on Compound and their stocks placed in a Uniswap collection. As time goes by, Nexus will continue growing beyond the smart agreement indemnity into other Crypto cover commodities.

Etherisc

Etherisc is constructing a platform for decentralized cover applications. The primary team established various shared infrastructure, commodities templates, and indemnity licenses. Moreover, the indemnity license permits every individual to generate indemnity commodities. Besides, the Etherisc public has designed a collection for primary indemnity commodities that ranges from flight delay indemnity to loaning collateral shield.

CDx

CDx is a platform for tokenized and tradeable indemnity swaps. Crypto capitalizers can safeguard their money from hacks on renowned exchanges. Exchange cover is among the essential indemnity commodities considering the many hacks in the past decade. The hacks lead to losses of significant funds in the capitalizers' investments. Moreover, CDx can be applied for various uses, including interchanging swaps for returns, shielding investors' crypto stocks, and staking against exchange safety.

Choosing Your Insurance Platform

Factors to Consider

Capital Pool and Liquidity

The significant variance with indemnity-like procedures is the mutual capital collection. The procedures permit sharing of dangers across various indemnities. The protocols also permit the collection to be under-collateralized; holds below a hundred percent of the total possible claim payments. The mutual collection efficiently insures dangers than the forecasting market and monetary derivatives insuring the same occurrence. This is because every marketplace or alternative is required to have the ability to payout personally hence requiring whole collateralization. Besides, the collection method can easily activate liquidity through many dangers. Instead of having liquidity for a two-sided marketplace, a particular side is occupied by the collection. The collection then offers liquidity to all dangers at once, and the central ceiling limits the extent of each danger.

Oracles

Nexus involves the voting technique hence a high similarity with Augur. However, other indemnity methods like Etherisc use an outside oracle as an information feed to decide claim payments. The monetary derivative lacks an oracle. The alternative purchaser can practice their right to purchase or retail at the predetermined value whenever they want to. It is a great advantage compared to the oracle method.

Flexibility

Forecast marketplace and monetary derivatives rapidly develop fresh commodities and take fresh dangers that fit their platform preference. The forecast markets are incredibly flexible and have the capability of deploying fresh commodities within a short period. Similarly, derivatives are fast to market, provided the danger lies within the overall standards and limitations of the platform. Indemnity commodities are slow and require plenty of study on valuing and underwriting to certify that the collection is comfortable taking the fresh danger. The flexibility of the danger being insured is a critical aspect to consider. When investors are using forecast markets and indemnity collections, they can only be restricted by their thoughts. However, monetary derivatives have more limitations since one must trade one financial stock for another at an open position. They are restricted by the financial stock that exists.

Pricing

The indemnity collection method has numerous advantages over the forecast market and derivatives methods when emphasizing extreme occurrences. For example, if the likelihood of an occurrence happening is one percent in a year, one can approximately get one percent of their capital. This is because the individual has to padlock the total possible claim value. Investment costs are a significant restricting aspect for the extreme occurrence, "deep out of the money occurrences," if whole collateralization is needed. Other events, "at the money risk," have a significant likelihood that a payoff will happen. In this case, investment costs are less critical than damages costs and flexibility of forecast markets and derivatives successes. Moreover, suppose individuals seek to hedge their dangers to smoothen their gains or cap their downside in unstable marketplaces. In that case, they should go for forecast markets and derivatives.

Every method functions better in specific conditions. Therefore, an individual should comprehend the suitable method to tackle the issue they are attempting to resolve. One can go ahead to dividing the elements into two for better comprehension of the best action to take:

- Possibility of the event happening.

- Results of assuming the event happens.

Blockchain is elevating the internet evolution to a higher level with decentralization. As the embracement of technology grows, many individuals recognize the advantages of a devolved ecosystem. The fashion, real estate, supply chain, and indemnity firms are discovering inventive methods of presenting the blockchain. Crypto indemnity for smart agreements and collateral loans provides an added layer of safety for beginners in the crypto world. Devolved indemnity with the application of NFTs and actual-life use scenarios will transmute the industry in numerous means. Communication among all significant participants will be undisputable and apparent.

Have you realized that crypto and blockchain users are accumulating each day? This has been achieved by the new blockchain enterprise incorporations and extensive embracement of cryptocurrency. Blockchain knowledge has become very significant, and it is among the top researched skills on LinkedIn. If individuals capitalize on themselves and become authorized blockchain developers, they will gain a competitive advantage over other workers. One can get knowledge from various sources available online.

Chapter 10 - Pay Using DeFi

A Classic Money Transaction

Money acted as a medium of exchange between goods and services and emphasized how well it circulated in the market. Over the last few years, there has been a change in the financial industry. Payments have changed and so have money transactions from fiat currencies known as traditional finances to decentralized finance online and through mobile applications.

The future of finance is relatively technological, and DeFi is the first step towards that direction; it is faster, transparent, cheaper, and more reliable. As we discover more non-traditional methods of doing business and leading everyday lives, we should understand the "classical money transactions" and how they would occur. This is by online payments, bank transactions through credit and debit cards, and integration of traditional and non-traditional modes of payments.

Bank Transfers

Bank transfers cover a wide range of services from; credit transfers, cash payments, wire transfers to local and international banks and giro-payments. Bank transactions are the most common types of payments in many parts of the world. Consumers can access these services in one of the following methods:

- Phone banking is infamously known as telebanking

- Online banking

- Mailed payments forms to a bank

- In-person bank payments.

Bank transfers are made at the request/initiative of the buyer (customer), and the payments are pushed by the bank and deposited in the seller's account. This fact is of importance for these reasons:

• Customers must always instruct their banks to authenticate payments, so an order is not always a payment.

• Once payment is made, a customer cannot ask the bank to reverse it; they can only ask the seller to refund the money.

• Bank transfers are very safe, and they have no reversal risks; the merchant has to rely on a customer to initiate the payment; once that authority is given, they can fully expect their payments.

• Online banking does not change the fundamentals of bank transfers; the only difference is that it's faster.

Benefits and drawbacks of bank transfers for the seller

Bank transfers are used by customers who do not have credit cards or do not prefer to make payments through cards. The seller has these benefits when the payments have been initiated: Transactions are safe and secure, and there's no chance for them to be reversed; they are fully electronic and customer-friendly.

The disadvantages, however, are, there are potential delays in the payment process, and the transactions can only take place when the buyer gives an order.

PayPal Platform

As online shopping increases, you must understand how the money gets to you, and this comes in three easy steps; one, the customer pays. Secondly, the payment information is encrypted, and lastly, the money is authorized or not.

There are three players regarding the process of credit/debit card payments, whether by phone, online or in person. On one end, there is the merchant (business owner), then the customer, and thirdly a technology connecting both of you.

Online payments

Understanding the online payment process will help you make better and informed decisions regarding the business. For online transactions, there are four stages every transaction goes through.

Authorization is the initial phase, and as a cardholder initiates a sale and the seller requests authorization from their bank. For a bank to grant the finances, they look at the card's status; if there's enough money, the security of a card if it's stolen or not, and on these factors, payment is authorized or not.

Batching finances are paid in a batch. The merchants store up transaction data, and they are paid all at once, which is more effective. In case fraud is detected, all transactions are cancelled.

Clearing involves the payments of all the batched transactions by the card networks.

Funding is the last process where the seller gets paid by the buyer. Some fees are paid to complete a transaction.

The payment process takes about 24-48 hours just to be initiated. There are factors to be considered like the bank's specific policies, the time and weekday the transaction was initiated, the type of industry, and the risk levels involved. In case a seller realizes delays, they could always inquire.

Going With the New Normal

Artificial intelligence has made the changes in the financial industry more efficient. The next generation of financial markets is powered by blockchain that consumes big data. A massive shift has come from centralized payments to Decentralized Finance by using private keys that hold an individual's personal financial information, which the owner can access.

DeFi eliminates the need for third-party participants such as processors, trustees, organizations to validate and approve payments and has reduced staffing in the financial markets. It is more efficient and offers financial freedom to its users, and it has eliminated many struggles, such as keeping updated with institutional changes and passwords.

The DeFi Payment Platform has simplified the process of financial transactions by reducing the costs of transactions. Reduced time to make transactions and the process is swift compared to traditional financial systems. In no time, DeFi has become the future of finance; the DeFi platform comes with several benefits such as:

- Low costs of transactions that are enabled by technology.

- They are secure because of the blockchain network that has been built through cryptography.

- Payments have been made public, and it ensures that payments have no room for failure.

- Absolute elimination of intermediaries that offers financial freedom even from the government.

- Payments made on HashCash (a global software company that offers solutions for blockchains, AI, and Big Data) are transparent and secure with traceable records.

How does the cryptocurrency process work like?

As we get to debunk the process of how DeFi payments are achieved, it worth noting that there are two significant differences between traditional finance and cryptocurrency. One, the client pays through a digital wallet and not through a Debit/credit card. Secondly, payments are made through cryptocurrency and not Fiat currencies such as Dollars or Pounds.

A Digital Wallet is an app or software more like bank accounts that enable users to complete transactions and store currencies. There are two types of wallets; one, a single currency wallet that operates just one currency like bitcoin, and secondly, a multi-currency wallet with a range of coins as payment options.

Once a buyer pays in cryptocurrency, the seller receives the payment in cryptocurrency. They can decide whether to continue doing business in cryptocurrency or translate that money into Fiat currencies. Many currencies are operating in the crypto market in Bitcoin and Altcoins (alternatives for bitcoin).

Advantages and Disadvantages of cryptocurrency as a payment method

The advantages cut across the global market in that the payment method is high-speed and efficient. The process that would have taken traditional means around seven days now takes few seconds. The payments are cross-border as well, the fees are low and relevant, and transactions can't be reversed.

The cons, however, are a bit wanting as not all users and sellers possess a digital wallet. The redirection to a payment page is often frustrating for the user. The crypto market is volatile, and most often, it experiences fluctuations; hence it isn't stable.

Documents required accepting Crypto as payment.

Once you decide to start paying using Crypto, you need to open a merchant's account and find a trustworthy PSP (Payment Service Provider). To open a merchant account and start accepting payments in Crypto, here is a list of all the required documents.

• Certificate of incorporation that shows the main aspects of your company (name, address, type of incorporation.

• Certificate of incumbency that shows details of the owners and the positions they occupy.

• Signature and passport copies of all the owners of the company, all scanned

• An online PSP form on a website for application.

• A license issued by your country for trade.

• Your turnover amount and the bank one are linked to.

There are crypto-friendly payment companies such as WYRE, which facilitates cross-border payments and has partnered with big crypto coins to offer the best services. Wyre allows for payments through apps such as Apple Pay, credit cards, and Google Pay.

DeFi came into the market in 2019 and had since then attracted several investors; in China, it is known as Open Finance or Distributed Finance. DeFi brings this process of payment to the global financial table.

Funds are placed in a Smart Contract Address creating a transparent fund pool. The funds are distributed on a global ledger that can be accessed universally.

DeFi does not authenticate its users through personal documents, as traditional systems do, as it is time-consuming.

DeFi runs on codes and algorithms and adopts AI to collect financial data and service the market. These algorithms run this market.

Five Benefits of Decentralized Finance

Currently, billions in dollars have been locked in DeFi, and the liquidity pool keeps increasing by the day. The hype will be here to last; here are some reasons why DeFi will change the Global financial Market as we know it.

Transparency

Every transaction on the DeFi platform enabled by the blockchain is public and is visible to all verified users. Every protocol and form of trade is made known due to the codes they are built on.

Very secure

DeFi is built on blockchains to mean that any data recorded on one blockchain will be spread to other blocks to keep track. This makes it difficult for hackers to take control of the entire system. Traditional services are prone to theft as well; the difference is DeFi made sure to take care of that problem.

Traceability

DeFi operates on a blockchain built-in ethereum; these are blocks built upon blocks. Any transaction, purchase, or payment made from any block is spread on all blocks. If one block is hacked, the other blocks are used to reinstate all its functions. Likewise, if developers and users cannot trace a transaction, the block nodes are used to search for it. No activity goes unrecognized.

Real-Time Payments

Traditional finance payments took about 24-48 hours to process within the country and about seven days to process cross-border transactions. DeFi has enabled swift transactions as payments take relatively few seconds to accomplish both in-country and across the border.

Lower costs

Due to the elimination of intermediaries in transactions and long verification processes, transfer costs have been reduced to a reasonable amount. The fees are favorable for anyone across the globe.

No intermediaries

DeFi, unlike traditional services, does not rely on intermediaries such as courts and banks to make payments and exist. They have no third-party members who decide on how and when a client could use their finances. On the other hand, users have absolute control over their finances and how they are used and invested. Smart Contracts take place to ensure security and no fraud in transactions.

Accessibility

This bridged the gap between the poor and the rich and the developed countries and the developing countries. The services offered by DeFi can be accessed worldwide and by anybody who chooses to. It is cheaper and can be accessed anywhere as long as a user has an internet connection as it is a 24/7 economy.

Open-source and Permissionless

The code used in DeFi is open source, which has led to the creation of more dApps that have catapulted the growth of DeFi. Any changes made on the codes and blocks with the majority in the agreement are accepted without question.

DeFi has many more advantages, which circle back to financial freedom and absolute control of assets. The future of finance is slowly and surely being taken away from government entities and banks. DeFi also comes with its sets of disadvantages that this book will address in this book at great length. It would be illogical to air out just how great it is without looking at both sides of the coin.

Decentralized Payment Project You Must Know About

There is a recent payment project in the DeFi ecosystem called SABLIER that is transforming the market. Sablier is a protocol for real-time finance on the ethereum blockchain. It enables continuous, autonomous, and trustless; this project has enabled continuous salaries on Ethereum.

Sablier was launched and announced on Twitter as an ethereum dApp that employers can use to pay employees. An employer makes a one-time deposit, and the Sablier allocates the payments to each individual as allocated by the company. This new project provides users with options to run by when they don't have enough money and need emergency funds. It means continuously that an employer selects an option on when to pay employees, like once a month, once every two weeks, or once per a specific duration. Before the end of a payroll stream, an employer can get their funds back; Sablier is secure as it is run on Smart contracts.

Sablier is used in making payroll payments; this was an intelligent move to rope industries into DeFi and get them from making bank transactions as a mode of payment. Apart from salaries, this platform can be used to pay freelancers worldwide, pay for any subscriptions, and pay for daily services such as (rent, car packing, and speed tickets, taxes, and consultation services for lawyers and doctors.)

Mainframe Acquired Sablier

Mainstream acquired the Sablier protocol and supported it; it also left the protocol open for other users to build on top of it. Mainframe is a current protocol that allows investors to sell their debt for an increased purchasing power. Borrowers deposit their collateral and mint tokens that represent a debt obligation.

Lenders then buy the tokenized debt at a discount and wait to redeem them when maturity has been reached. Investors can also work with this protocol as guarantors; this earns them a fee considering which direction the market goes.

Why not combine

The start of decentralized finance was not welcomed by traditional finance, yet slowly some industries have started to accept that these two industries can coexist. On the other hand, some industries have chosen to remain dominantly on fiat currencies while others have entirely accepted Decentralized finance as the only means of trade and payments.

The CeFi and DeFi Bridge

The main goal of DeFi is to build a financial system that is Permissionless, open, and financial freedom. However, there are disadvantages to this system because there's no oversight, and anyone can launch a platform to raise money and probably squander people in the long run.

To improve the stability of cryptocurrencies, stablecoins were created and were created by joining cryptocurrency and fiat currencies. Here are examples of payment solutions that have accepted crypto assets and coins for payments.

Skrill

It was founded in 2001 as Moneybookers limited and later rebranded as Skrill. It created a Skrill Digital wallet for its users in more than 30 countries and allows them to trade in Bitcoin, Ethereum, Litecoin, and Bitcoin Cash, among other cryptocurrencies. It partnered up with an unnamed exchange to facilitate its conversion between cryptocurrencies and over 40 fiat currencies.

PayPal

In mid-2015, PayPal partnered with a few crypto exchanges such as Coinbase and Gocoin to enable deposits and withdrawals of cryptocurrencies. PayPal has been seen to be Pro-Blockchain in the current market as it once filled a patent to increase crypto payments speed through using secondary private keys.

Credit Card

Big credit card names in the industry, such as Visa and MasterCard, and several banks have banned the use of crypto purchases altogether. Crypto users can, however, access a third party like Simplex to enable them to use these services. It is an Israeli-based company that allows traders to pay using credit cards through algorithms that eliminate all fraud and offer protection from Chargebacks.

The New Norm

DeFi has made purchasing in cryptocurrency much easier than it was ten years ago. Many more industries globally accept Crypto as a mode of payment and purchase in the wake of the new decade. In a short period, cryptocurrency has been in the market. It is gaining more substantial grounds; if the Centralized Finance and Decentralized Finance can get more ways to coexist, many global citizens would be happy.

Chapter 11 - Lending your Assets

Several firms have commenced experimenting with Blockchain's potential. The economic sector has presented the necessity to construct blockchain-founded fintech protocols. Blockchain is aimed at transforming the traditional monetary network. The evolution can happen if the Blockchain covers almost every financial service, from online payouts to crypto swapping. Despite the excitement already present in the marketplace, DeFi continues to develop, attracting significant capital amounts. Maker, Compound, and Aave are the directors of DeFi Lending. The leaders regard themselves as the individuals' priorities when purchasing DeFi tokens. The concepts illustrated below explains why DeFi lending has become famous:

DeFi Lending and Borrowing: What is it?

DeFi lending platforms are purposed for providing cryptocurrency loans in a trustless way. The means do not require intermediaries, and individuals are permitted to register their cryptocurrencies on the platform for loaning purposes. P2P lending platform allows borrowers to acquire a loan without intermediaries' involvement. Moreover, the lending platform also permits individuals to get interests. DeFi is the leading DApp in terms of loaning growth rate, and it is the major contributor for padlocking crypto stocks.

Why Should I Even Lend?

Benefits of Lending

a. Accessibility

Crypto lending is more accessible compared to loaning from a traditional bank. Traditional banks involve a length procedure, and an individual's credit score is considered when determining the amount of money a person can borrow. Besides, in a traditional bank, other aspects such as credit history and revenue are considered. However, in Crypto lending, an individual is not required to have a bank account, and in most crypto loaning platforms, an individual's credit score isn't considered. Crypto loans aids individuals to acquire the money they need when traditional banks cannot give them loans. Crypto lending has made loans more accessible and given many individuals economic freedom.

b. Lower Charges

The traditional banks charge enormous fees for different services, such as the conversion of currencies. In cryptocurrency loaning, the fees are clearly outlined and usually are less than those of banks. Generally, an individual is only required to pay only one service charge, and if they need to be paid in a varying coinage, the exchange rates charged are affordable. Moreover, most crypto loaning platforms offer different alternatives of the currencies they prefer to be paid out in. Some offer both fiat coinage and stablecoins, while others give cryptocurrency. An individual can withdraw their funds into whichever currency they want to; no restrictions.

c. Flexible Loan Terms

The banks determine the amount of money they can lend to an individual and the interest rate to be charged. Cryptocurrency loans allow individuals to determine the duration before loan payment, loan-to-value ratio, and the fiat coinage they want to be paid out in. The amount of loan an individual gets is determined by their security, and other conditions are straightforward. Moreover, some lending platforms do not charge minimum monthly payouts if the loan is entirely paid by the end of the agreed duration. Other platforms give lower rates of interest if an individual pays the loan in a particular cryptocurrency.

d. Safety

Most banks have been involved in theft scandals hence making individuals question the safety of their money. Banks are naturally imperfect and do not have suitable safety measures, especially the technology used. Crypto loaning platforms are more secure than banks. The lending platforms enlist their safety measures on their online sites. They also explain how they safeguard individuals' collaterals and store most of the individuals' funds in cold wallets. The cold wallets store the funds offline, and it is impossible to hack. Moreover, some renowned crypto loaning platforms insure all the digital stocks on the platform.

e. Speed

The conventional method takes a long time before a loan is approved. Some even take a week, while others can process a loan within a day, although several aspects have to be considered. Crypto loaning platforms approve a loan within a day. The loaning platforms only require an identification card to approve a loan. If individuals have an identification card and some cryptocurrency that they can deposit as security, they are qualified for a loan. However, the loan approval might take a bit longer if it is a P2P system that requires one to locate a loaner. The P2P system requires coordination from both lenders and borrowers; hence, individuals seeking fast loans should try getting one from other platforms.

You Can also Borrow if Necessary

Why should One Borrow?

Loss management due to value volatility

The possible increase in cryptocurrencies' values has made retailing or the use of digital currencies less attractive. Holding cryptocurrencies is currently a suitable alternative. Some DeFi platforms like Nuo Network allow holders to borrow digital stocks for their daily usage without surrendering possession of their crypto coins. Most people wonder how investors make their crypto coins usable and applicable without retailing them or using them to purchase an item. The investors either pledge the cryptocurrencies as security to acquire loans or use the digital stocks safeguarded to lend for their everyday necessities.

Moreover, when investors borrow money, they control the danger exposed to their stocks and acquire funds without retailing their holdings. Nuo provides higher-price collateral. Nuo decreases the danger of borrowing and also permits individuals to borrow at reduced interest rates. Collateralization encourages borrowers to pay their loans on time to avoid a part of their security being sold to compensate for the loan.

Crypto Hedging

It is a method adopted by investors to curb risks related to marketplace volatility hence maximizing their returns. Crypto hedging involves taking a balancing position on digital stocks. Through short retailing, investors can get some returns and also maintain possession of their digital currencies. Short selling involves the exercise of borrowing digital stocks and retailing them with the expectation that prices will fall. Therefore, investors registered with the DeFi platform can engage in profitable short selling by directly borrowing digital stocks from loaners and retailing them when prices are anticipated to drop. Margin swapping alternative is available for investors with restricted crypto stocks. DeFi platform like Nuo permits borrowers to use up to three times leverage and investors can short retail loaned digital stocks. Besides, investors can loan their cryptocurrencies they hold to individuals instead of keeping them in folders waiting for the marketplace to go upwards.

Circumstances of Borrowing

Different Crypto loaning platforms give varying sets of requirements to individuals who are willing to borrow funds. For example, Collateralized Borrowing and Lending Platform based in India has several requirements for acquiring a loan. In this case, the individuals willing to borrow must submit their proposals in the CBLO auction marketplace opened at a specific timeframe. The bid should have the amount of money and the interest rate to be charged, and it can be annulled at any time during the open period. Unfortunately, borrowers cannot alter their bids after submission, and after the auction period is closed, the CBLO proposals are matched with what the software is offering. The prosperous borrowers are then notified, and the unsuccessful individuals can submit their proposals in the CBLO usual marketplace. The CCIL takes the responsibility of the primary counterparty and assures payment of the deals.

Risks of Borrowing Assets

An individual is required to give collateral that is padlocked in a smart contract before they are termed eligible for a loan. The security preferred is either a blockchain stock or a token. One can receive a loan in the form of a different blockchain stock from the collateral one. For instance, in a Compound platform, an individual who has padlocked Ethereum as the collateral can receive a loan in the form of DAI. Besides, one can borrow up to seventy-five percent of their collateral worth. Considering the high volatility of most crypto stocks, an individual faces the danger of being liquidated. This indicates that if the worth of ETH in the market decreases significantly, the padlocked ETH will be valued less than the loan the individual took. The personal losses the security, but the loan is termed as settled.

Collateralized Borrowing

It is a form of borrowing adapted by all decentralized lending platforms. Collateralized borrowing indicates that the borrower must padlock security of higher worth than the worth of borrowing. The security ensures that loaners are reimbursed even if the borrower defaults on the loan agreement. Collateral borrowing considers the concept of liquidation when carrying out loaning procedures. In this case, liquidation occurs when an individual's loan is automatically refunded by retailing some of their security to purchase back the stick they owe their loaner. Besides, liquidation occurs when a person's borrow reduces below the needed level of collateralization; ranges from 115% to 150%.

How Does DeFi Lending and Borrowing Work?

DeFi protocols function by eliminating the intermediaries in the lending and borrowing deals. The app gathers cash from investors who have more than they require at the moment and loans it to individuals who require the funds. A smart contract on the Blockchain controls the whole procedure. This indicates that no individual is controlling the software, especially the funds being interchanged. A smart algorithm's interest rates are determined by relying on the information it gets from the marketplace; demand and supply volumes. Some of the DeFi platforms include Compound Finance, Dy/Dx, MakerDAO, and Fulcrum. The platforms produce plenty of money based on the loans offered.

The Process

We can use a popular crypto loaning platform like MakerDAO to illustrate the process of lending and borrowing Crypto assets.

An individual sends Ethereum to their favorite ETH wallets, such as Trezor and Metamask.

The borrower then visits the Collateralized Debt Portal and links to the folder they sent their ETH to.

The individual then clicks the "Open CDP" button to analyze the amount of DAI they want and Ethereum they are willing to post as their security.

After analyzing the conditions, an individual can click "Collateralized & Generate," and immediately their Ethereum is posted as security in the list of freshly issued DAI.

The Impact Is Not Solely on You

a) Financial Information

A set of stakeholders manages information within the monetary markets. The stakeholders monitor the value, accessibility, and type of information being offered. Decentralized Finance will aid in democratizing information, determining how information is supplied and presented, and generate prize networks that encourage marketplace participants. A firm known as DIA is targeting becoming the open-source Bloomberg for both cryptocurrencies and traditional banks. Its platform uses crypto-based monetary incentives to drive supply and adaptability of apparent crowd-confirmed value information and oracles on digital and monetary stocks. Monetary organizations which adopt DIA will get an immutable and authenticated sole source of economic marketplace information for any market and stock kind.

b) Lending

DeFi loaning permits apparent and safe protocols to source funds that are incentivized with different crypto prizes. DeFi has led to the invention of non-collateral loans, compounding of interest rates, and P2P lending that aids in getting rid of mediators. DeFi continues to develop as firms leverage the industry's composability. The composability permits applications to combine and construct on top of each other, generating an extended system effect. Moreover, the open-source method promotes invention and inspires fair competition.

c) Decentralized Exchanges

DEX platforms permit individuals to be in control of their funds kept in external folders. This reduces the danger of depositing crypto into exchanges, leading to massive loss of their capital if the exchanges are hacked. The decentralized exchanges continue to develop and are presently acquiring market share from many traditional centralized exchanges. Generally, the regulatory challenges could make this a delayed procedure, but the industry specialists have faith in how DeFi manages their stocks.

d) Asset Management

DeFi gives different benefits when it comes to stock management. Some of the advantages include;

- Automation

- Non-custodial stocks possession

- Universal accessibility

- Financial inclusion and account-anonymity

DeFi commodities are evolving quickly to become easier to use and knowledgeable to aid in educating individuals on how to control their stocks within the industry efficiently.

Four Lending Platforms to Look Into

1) Aave

The loaning platform regards itself as the marketplace leader after it evolved from LEND to AAVE and the introduction of Aave V2. The platform uses tokens that trace interest gained in actual time. Besides, Aave leverages AAVE, an inborn token for administration, and it is risked as the cover against shortfall occurrences in an interchange for prizes.

Benefits of lending on Aave

It supports more than twenty varying cryptocurrencies hence offering diversity to lenders and borrowers.

It offers an inborn token; AAVE, which can be obtained through betting

It supports particular security types such as Uniswap LP tokens and TokenSets.

Individuals can repay the loan immediately using the security instead of purchasing the borrowed stock and repaying the loan manually.

Individuals can use Swap Rate to padlock a fixed profit on aDAI for a predetermined period.

2) Compound Finance

It is a permissionless loaning platform that uses inbuilt tokens known as cTokens. Every stock has its personal cToken such as Cdai and Cusd, which traces possession and collects interest across their respective loaning pools.

Compound Finance is similar to other lending platforms in that it provides enormous gains on stablecoins such as DAI and USDC.

Benefits of Lending on Compound

It features COMP, a governance token that is obtained by loaning stocks on Compound.

Individuals can buy indemnity on Compound smart contracts using Nexus Mutual.

Individuals can use Opyn to buy alternatives on cTokens

It is consolidated into renowned stock management dashboards such as InstaDapp and Zerion

The cTokens can be used to buy Yield Sets on Set Protocol.

3) DYdX

The platform permits individuals to open margin extended or petite positions on Ethereum and USDC with up to five times leverage. Besides, DEX, the surging decentralized exchange, offers cross-margin loaning and borrowing. This indicates that individuals can get passive revenue while supported stocks remain in the exchange contract. The platform also supports permanent futures swapping with higher leverage which has grown to the Starkware Layer.

Benefits of lending on dYdX

The funds supplied on dYdX gather interest even when one is using it to trade.

Individuals can buy smart contract insurances on dYdX using Nexus

Mutual.

Dharma

It is a customer-facing mobile application that emphasizes making loaning more available and probable. It offers a bridge from individuals' fiat bank accounts to the Decentralized Finance universe, leveraging many DeFi platforms to loan and borrow funds. Some of the protocols included in the leverage are Compound, Aave, and Yearn.

Benefits of lending on Dharma

It provides a mobile-first method. Their commodities are available on Android applications stores, and it is a bit intuitive to fresh individuals.

It provides a fiat on-ramp by permitting individuals to trade from USD to USDC stablecoin rapidly.

The application permits individuals to supply renowned DeFi protocols even if they don't have any technical knowledge.

The above illustrated concepts indicate that DeFi lending has a high possibility of reshaping the whole monetary ecosystem. DeFi lending tries to devolve the primary traditional monetary services such as payouts, swapping, investments, indemnity, loaning, and borrowing. Besides, DeFi lending is involved with the fascinating technology; hence it possesses massive opportunities of revolutionizing the universal monetary landscape.

Chapter 12 - Wait, What? There is a Lottery?

The year 2020 is regarded as the year of Decentralized Finance. Cryptocurrency lottery played a significant role in the scaling of the fresh era of crypto stocks. The industry witnessed a continuous increase in the number of individuals risking crypto to get fixed interests or reap farming rewards. The surge led to a decrease of miners in PoW; proof-of-work Blockchain. Besides, Crypto valued at approximately a billion dollars has been risked in Kraken's platforms. Other primary exchanges such as Binance and Huobi have also held vast amounts of staked Crypto. In the report given in January 2021, the sum of stocks risked in DeFi platforms is approximately twenty-three billion dollars. The report points to a further rise in crypto staking demand.

The Answer is YES

Meaning of Decentralized Lottery

The decentralized lottery is the exercise where individuals padlock their funds in crypto wallets. The funds are used in participating in the maintenance of PoS; Proof-of-Stake functions based on the blockchain software. It resembles crypto mining since it aids a system to accomplish an agreement while recompensing individuals involved.

Concept behind it

In betting, the right to authenticate deals is founded on the number of coins held in a folder. However, the same as mining in Proof-of-Work, individuals are encouraged to get a new block or add a deal on a blockchain. Not only are PoS blockchain podiums scalable, but they also have incredible deal speeds.

Pros

a) For Riskers

- A simple way of earning passive revenue.

- The risking platforms charge low entry fees.

- Returns in interest rates might be greater than the riskers' expectations.

- The platforms are highly safe with the aid of smart contracts.

- Very easy for beginners to start risking in DeFi.

b) For Risking Platforms

- **Offers the risking platforms more liquidity**
- **The platforms earn incomes from both riskers and token systems.**
- **The platforms can access energetic cryptocurrency banks.**

Cons

Lack of on-chain resolutions for creating randomness in a smart contract.

Unfair distribution of funds

Unavailability of the largest lotteries to all individuals from various nations.

The stakers often question the fairness of the lotteries.

Risk of Decentralized Lottery

Manipulation

Lottery players always have many questions regarding the fairness of the lottery platform they are using. Some of the questions include;

Are the deals and coupons real?

After how long are rewards paid?

Is the random digit generator method safe and arbitrary?

Is the jackpot winner real?

Generally, players face the risk of manipulation, which is evident in centralized lotteries. For example:

❖ Hot Lotto Fraud Scandal

A former data safety manager at American Multi-State Lottery Association (AMLA) confirmed that he and two other individuals had rigged RNG. The manager installed a network code that allowed him to adjust RNG and guess victory digits on particular dates of the year. He was able to win a fourteen million dollar jackpot in 2010.

❖ The 1980 Pennsylvania Lottery Scandal

The scandal involved rigging of the daily digit. The number included three digits with an omission of digits four and six, and all the balls in the three pieces were weighted. It was clear that the winning figure would be a merge of 4s and 6s. Six hundred sixty-six turned out to be the winning figure, but the winners were never rewarded, and the principal conspirators were jailed.

Distribution of funds

In most scenarios, lotteries are meant for helping the less fortunate and communal projects. However, players can question the equitable distribution of funds, especially in highly corrupted nations. There is no means of getting adequate information about funds distribution, making it difficult for stakers to trust a particular lottery association.

Availability

The rural marketplaces are small in size, limiting players from participating in large lotteries in the universe. Although the new online resolutions allow participants to buy worldwide lottery coupons, the amenity charges, risks of scams, and mismanagements are still high. Currently, the state rules manage how lotteries are operated in various parts of the universe. Less than fifty percent of the total money collected from coupon sales is given to the reward pool. Moreover, lottery players have no power over the amount of cash gathered from coupon sales, and some nations tax lottery winnings.

Looking into how it Works

An individual is required to hold cryptocurrency for them to padlock it in a smart contract. When the betters' stakes are padlocked, they vote for deals approval. The contract between the risker and the blockchain system functions, and the betting regulations are different on various systems. Some of the rules include:

The risker consents that they will only authenticate valid deals on the system. For instance, the individuals will not validate double-spend deals.

In the swap for accepting confirmed deals, the system recompenses the risker with a reward.

If a risker vote to authenticate illegal deals, the stakers might lose some or the whole amount of their stake.

The protocol is more straightforward than mining which needs plenty of computing equipment and energy for providing Proof-of-Work. Authenticators get a reward from the system for padlocking their cryptocurrency to achieve consensus. The regulations explaining the mechanical and monetary requirements act as the authenticators.

Risking Reward Network

The compensations are calculated with algorithms and dispersed across the stakes involved in the authentication of the deals. Besides, each system has its regulations depending on the following:

• Amount of the risked stocks in a system.

- The amount of risked assets by the stakers

- **The risking duration**

- **The rate of inflation**

- **System's rate of assurance.**

Exploring how it is made

There are three technology elements involved in the blockchain lottery protocol; public Blockchain, web platforms for stakers, and web platform managers.

Process of making Lottery Protocols

a. Stakers register themselves in the staking platform

Riskers are required to sign up to engage in the lottery and attain membership. The data required when signing up includes; name, folder address, email identification, and mobile number. After the registration is successful, stakers get signals and announcements associated with coupon openings regularly.

b. Announcement of coupon openings and deployment of smart contracts by the managers.

The managers announce the coupon openings on the podium. The notifications are then sent to the stakers. Besides, the admins also position smart contracts that consist of pre-described regulations for the staking game. The rules bring impartiality and transparency to the network. Smart contracts determine the data to be shared with participants in the network hence enhancing confidentiality of the information. The identification of the riskers remains unknown since they buy coupons using cryptocurrencies. The deals kept in the communal blockchain permit traceability and made resolving disputes associated with staking easier.

c. Generation of an arbitrary digit which is noted down on the Blockchain.

The arbitrary digit generator is founded on the Blockchain. The algorithm depends on current arbitrary blockchain deals. The algorithm pulls a particular order of digits to create every winning figure sequence. Since no one knows the next deal in the Blockchain, the staking platform adds another level of arbitrariness to the choosing procedure. After the arbitrary digit creation and its matching with the risker's coupon number, they are rewarded. The cash is mechanically sent to their respective folders.

The money to be distributed to stakers is explained in the smart contract. Therefore, the decided commissions and cash are given to each risker on the platform. Besides, the smart contract code is accessible publicly on the podium. The publicity permits players to examine the regulations defined in the contracts and pick whether the funds are dispersed impartially.

d. Stakers can trace the Past of Registers of the Deals.

The tracing allows the stakers to view who won jackpots in the past. Moreover, the stakers can view if the commissions and victories are salaried, as illustrated in the smart agreements.

Why do People make them?

Constructing a decentralized lottery only requires several contracts. The contracts are in code form, and they are simple to spin up. The use of VRF, Chainlink Verifiable Random Function, makes it simple to manage while certifying it is safe, continuous, and provably arbitrary. There are various reasons why people construct decentralized lottery:

a) Incorruptible

Recent lotteries require an individual to have faith that the operators of the lottery platform are running it genuinely. Unfortunately, there have been several incidents where lotteries have been rigged. A staker should not have worries about such scenarios. To curb such occurrences, blockchain lotteries have come up with platforms that cannot be attacked or corrupted. In the platforms, digits are selected arbitrarily, and every individual can prove that. Therefore, lotteries are better off on blockchains since the significant part of every lottery is the trust players have that their money will be safe and handled fairly.

b) Lower Overheads

The centralized lotteries experience plenty of overhead costs such as:

- Personnel to manage the lottery servers

- Personnel to manage coupons and packaging

- Payment of television and radio draws as well as online ads.

Decentralized lotteries can solve some of the above challenges. After the contract is created and approved to be safe, one cannot reverse that. One can only deploy a front-end on a similar openly-acquired lottery smart contract. After the procedure, the servers are now substituted with the Blockchain.

Lottery Platforms Worth Checking Out

a. Pool2Gether

The Pool2Gether is a no-loss cash game founded on ETH. It functions straightforwardly. The first step involves individual purchasing coupons by depositing in any reward collection. They get one coupon for each dollar deposited. The player is eligible to win prizes if they continue storing their cash deposited in the collection. The rewards are from the interest received on all the funds deposited in the collection. Besides, an individual can never experience loss since they can withdraw their money at any time.

b. ICONbet DAOLottery

ICONbet is the initial Decentralized Autonomous Organization. It is based on the ICON system, and it is a staking platform engrossed in playing competitions. The objective of the ICONbet personnel is that its layout will transform from an originally centralized to a Decentralized Autonomous Organization as time passes. The transformation can be done by the circulation of tokens holding the platform's ownership. Moreover, the TAP Tokens are used for DAO votes that shape the generation of the ICONbet platform.

c. $IC X Staking Lossless Lottery

The platform is formed on the ICON system. In the PoS, interests are produced by padlocking digital stocks. In this case, players can purchase coupons by padlocking ICX stocks in a smart contract placed on the ICON Blockchain. The padlocked tokens then produce interest through betting. In every draw, a single winner is awarded the total earned betting interest. Besides, participants can quit the lottery and redeem their coupons for their $ICX worth.

d. PancakeSwap

It is a decentralized mechanized market creator that is operating on the Binance Smart Chain. The platform allows individuals to trade between tokens on the BSC chain and get $CAKE tokens through farming. Moreover, the platform consists of a lottery featuring pancakes and rabbits, making it more appealing than the common lottery. If a player wants to win the lottery's biggest jackpot, they are required to match the four digits on their coupon with the position of the four winning digits. Similarly, if a player only matches two digits, they will still receive a prize.

e. MOS Lottery

The blockchain-founded lottery network was generated to solve the challenges inherited in the lottery marketplace today. It has recently introduced its platform, and this provides fresh ways of betting on asset prices. Through the intelligent blockchain-founded Ether contract, all the stakes and outcomes are performed publicly in the network. The outcomes are also recorded on the mutual ledger without outsiders' involvement.

Firms get improved by the aid of the DeFi grounded lottery working network. The players are assured that they won't incur losses, leading to increased participants in the apparent platforms. Business managers and generally anyone can start their decentralized lottery platform rapidly with the aid of the developers. Various firms have skilled tech developers who give well-organized and complete lottery network development services. You might be the next decentralized lottery owner; visit the online sites and get more knowledge.

Chapter 13 - Let's Talk About Management

You don't have to manage it by yourself

Asset management ranks on the list of solutions offered by decentralised finance (DeFi). On many occasions, investors in the traditional market have overlooked their investment potential due to various factors. To some, they can afford service costs and arising risks and reside in areas that provide investment opportunities within the financial market.

When it comes to decentralized asset management, every investor has a chance to access a broader range of investment opportunities rather than the traditional finance model that appears prohibitive to many of them.

Investment bankers or specialized institutions can modify an investment portfolio to specific features, for instance, goals, income, or risk profiles. However, asset management companies control this process, while investors encounter restrictions when accessing their accounts. Also, they have to pay fees to third parties, implying that investors have little autonomy over their assets.

What is asset management?

Asset management is the process of creating, running, maintaining, and selling assets in an economical way. In finance, it refers to companies or individuals who manage assets on account of the investor or other organizations.

A company has to track its assets time and again, enabling shareholders to determine the available assets that can generate maximum yields. In asset management, many managers encounter challenges such as the role of the asset management process in the business or devising ways to create a better asset management plan.

Pros of DeFi asset management

DeFi has transformed asset management services especially providing affordable methods and more access to investment opportunities. For example, it removes the necessity for managers. In the DeFi ecosystem, products under asset management are non-custodial, implying that users don't have to transfer funds or share their private keys. Since services are automated in DeFi projects, liquidations and collateralization appear smooth and faster.

Transparency

With decentralized tech at its core, DeFi asset management offers a transparent process. In contrast, transparency is a dim feature within traditional finance since settlements can take a more prolonged period. In addition, companies' reports are published once each quarter, placing shareholders in a tough spot when they seek clarity about their assets. The advancement of robust blockchain technology aims to allow investors to access their assets' information whenever they wish.

Composability

Another merit that comes with DeFi asset management is composability. Investors can make use of hyper customization and get enough space for personalization based on growth, income, and liquidity levels. The exciting part is that investors from all corners of the world can access these benefits. Thus, despite ethnicity or locality, anyone has a chance to manage their investment portfolios.

Cons of DeFi asset management

DeFi asset management has a downside that is based on the underlying blockchain technology.

Uncertainty

When DeFi projects are built on an unstable blockchain, the project will likely inherit the flaws from the host blockchain. With the current upgrade of Ethereum blockchain, any mistake that would occur when shifting from PoW to the novel Eth 2.0 PoS can pose a significant risk to DeFi projects.

Over-collateralization

Issuance of crypto loans is a booming service in the DeFi ecosystem. However, this service is prone to over-collateralization. In several cases, it happens if the borrowed asset is higher than the loan amount. In general, Defi projects tend to have increased collateralization to help navigate the removal of barriers like credit rating.

Scalability

One more issue facing DeFi projects is the scalability of the host blockchain. These issues arise when it takes long intervals to process a transaction. Also, network congestion can render transactions quite expensive.

Five important characteristics of assets management

The following are major asset management features.

Globally accessible

Anyone has a chance to access asset management tools despite their ethnicity or area of residence.

Non-custodial

Possession of assets under non-custodial terms is never revoked. Therefore, these assets will continue being held on the wallet in use.

Automated

At the moment, many asset management tools are embracing automation, making collateralization, liquidations, and rebalances more effortless and smooth. Also, automated services remove the necessity of user interaction.

Pseudo-anonymous

Since asset management products connect via wallet address, users who seek privacy can remain anonymous.

Composable

Several asset management projects connect to different DeFi projects, which helps create a thrilling DeFi experience.

Exploring how asset management works

Asset management is considered a fundamental process that helps manage organizational records and hardware assets. The process involves strategic planning for an organization and its environs to minimize costs and address other significant gains.

An asset management system will enable business accounts to handle and track different assets like machines, computers, and equipment being used within an organization.

How the asset management process takes place

The asset management process involves a number of steps, and they follow below.

Add assets

Assets can be added using two methods. One is manually, and the other is by importing using a predefined excel or CSV template file. However, only the authorized user can add assets to the asset management by entering the data needed.

Add assets from other applications

If an organization plans to switch from its current asset management application to another application, such as Asset Infinity's asset management software, it can make a move with ease. Moreover, the asset information will remain tamper-proof in the process.

Many organizations have taken a further step to create special ID codes for their assets that have to be scanned and receive their corresponding details.

Change in assets details

Some details may be omitted after discarding or adding an asset. You can record or add new data by editing and modifying the earlier entered asset details.

With this option, you can adjust the asset details if the asset has been added and the details moved to General Ledger.

Transfer of assets

The transfer option enables the transfer of an asset to another destination, such as a department or between individuals. However, there are factors to consider before the transfer of assets. For example, authorities have to determine if they plan to move the entire asset or multiple assets. The transfer process can begin via a handheld device or through a web-based asset management application.

Asset Reports

The asset management application will provide you with a variety of options to generate reports based on the overall inventory transactions, transfer of assets, depreciation or appreciation reports, and the life-cycle cost of the asset.

You can choose to generate these reports monthly or quarterly to receive important information about the asset. On the other hand, the email option is available to get these reports depending on your set time frame.

Disposal of assets

There is a discard option that allows the disposal of an individual or multiple assets. Nonetheless, the net asset value will determine the overall amount relating to the discarded asset.

How these can keep track of your assets

An effective asset management process will assist in running a business effectively and have better control of the operations. Still, it will provide many advantages to an organization, such as extensive data analysis and real-time data collection. In addition, there are other solutions addressed in the process, and they include:

Real-time asset tracking

Assets are an essential part of any business. However, based on how you manage them, they can increase, depreciate, or even varnish. Therefore, real-time asset tracking appears vital in an asset management process.

Attain total accuracy

You can quickly notice when an asset is misplaced or requires maintenance. Also, you can generate accurate and thorough audit reports. Installing a robust system can help track all the asset information and history regardless of the business size.

Determine ghost assets

Some assets can get stolen, or the details are not correctly entered and still appear in the system. Asset management system with features such as real-time tracking will assist remove such ghost assets within the system.

Improved efficiency

The asset management process enables a business owner to learn the function of every asset within the business sector. This means understanding their potential, finding better ways of running them, and generating a thorough Return on Investment report. The owner will then determine if they need to get disposed of to reduce the costs.

Identify the business patterns

Like operations and predictions, an asset management system will enable the owner to understand his/her assets better and identify the business patterns. In addition, the owner can learn more about the asset life cycle and plan for maintenance easily, which is essential to address the flaws before they lead to a bigger problem.

Non-custodial characteristics of an asset management platform

Beginners within the crypto space may encounter a challenging moment understanding the fundamental concepts. You can learn many things, but first, you should identify convenient ways of keeping your assets safe. A decade ago, only a few platforms provided exchange and wallet services.

However, the advancement of blockchain technology has facilitated the development of better and secure platforms that offer crypto services.

Still, several beginners find it difficult to distinguish between custodial and non-custodial services. So today, we will address non-custodial services. Assets under the non-custodial category mean that their ownership is never revoked.

Non-custodial platforms allow their users to own private keys, which is considered safer if the platform encounters a data breach or other security-related threats.

Users using non-custodial platforms have complete control over their funds. For example, if you own a cryptocurrency in a non-custodial wallet, this will allow you complete autonomy over your asset. There are many non-custodial wallets such as Bitcoin.com client, Electron Cash, and Jaxx.

Are my assets safe?

Safety starts with you. Since non-custodial wallets allow users complete autonomy, they are responsible for the safety of their accounts and private keys.

Although non-custodial services are considered safer, you can likely lose your private key or misplace it. Therefore, it's considered a wise move to learn better ways of keeping your private key safe to achieve financial independence.

Recommended Asset management projects

The following projects appear suitable to help hedge risks and manage DeFi exposure in 2021.

Set protocol

One of the leading asset management products is the Set protocol, enabling users to utilize complex trading strategies by buying sets (ERC20 tokens).

Set protocol sums several automated trading strategies into a detailed list that rebalances topics to distinct technical indicators and patterns such as Relative Strength Index and Moving Averages.

The Set Protocol was first developed in 2018. Later, it was launched through Ethereum mainnet in April 2019. Set labs, an SF-based company, has outstanding product strategists. The team of developers like Anthony Sassano and Felix Fang have great experience and reputation. Others like CTO Alex Soong and CPO Inje Yeo have contributed to startups such as 21.com, Apple, and Square.

Importance of Set Protocol

- Yield sets use compound cTokens, implying that users can generate passive income from interest-earning assets if the set appears stable.

- The Set Protocol provides trades an opportunity to share trading strategies via Social Trader. Also, other users can pursue the same trading tactics just like experienced traders with just a click.

- Account Dashboard or DeFisharp can assist manage Set positions with much ease.

Zapper

Zapper is considered a one-stop shop that helps to deploy and manage DeFi projects. Zapper comes with many benefits, such as minimizing costs and time, including the hassle of managing positions within various DeFi projects. Eventually, this helps fragmentation by developing a central, non-custodial dashboard to shift among leading income streams. In addition, Zapper users can take advantage of custom smart contracts to deploy capital, which minimizes the costs. At the same time, users can convert ETH tokens to the essentials positions within any platform.

The merger between DeFiZap and DeFiSnap led to the emergence of Zapper. These two asset management tools came together to provide an efficient DeFi interface in the market.

If you're new to DeFiZap, the project was developed by the Kyber DeFi Virtual hackathon. With DeFizap, users could easily take advantage of zaps to deploy capital into various income-generating activities, for instance, Uniswap liquidity pools.

On the other hand, DeFiSnap assists in tracking DeFi positions within the leading protocols such as Set Protocol, Compound, Synthetix. DeFiSnap is among the leading grant recipients of Gitcoin Grants Round 5. DeFiSnap has earned prestige for having an immense amount of DeFi integrations in the asset management ecosystem. Although users could not deploy capital through DeFiSnap, it can help track prime positions within various sectors such as liquidity pools, investments, and wallets.

Importance of Zapper

• You can easily track debt owned within DeFi products to determine the positions that require supplements.

• The Protocol Allocation tool can help observe how DeFi positions are spread out based on percentage.

• You can track how various positions will perform with ROI forecasts.

• You can use Pool Pipes to bridge capital between various liquidity pools.

Zerion

As an interface of DeFi, Zerion enables users to invest, buy, sell, lend or even borrow assets. Zerion users have a chance to manage their DeFi portfolio within various accounts. Still, they can track their assets easily using push notifications and live price updates.

Zerion's primary goal is to empower the global population with transparent, productive, and autonomous financial services. The platform was developed by CEO Evgeny Yurtaev and COO Vadim Koleoshkin, who funded it during the first two years.

Zerion has a user-friendly interface that offers access to the open protocols of DeFi. Although ease of use is limiting DeFi adoption, Zerion aims to address this through its platform. Furthermore, Zerion is gaining a reputation within the masses since it is non-custodial, offers easy global access, and personal information is not essential.

Zerion has originated $19 million worthy transactions, processed around $16 million compound deposits, provided $2 million liquidity to Uniswap in a month, and won the best UX award in the Ethereum ecosystem at Devcon 5 from its launch to December 2019.

Importance of Zerion

- With a QR code, users can link their Zerion dashboard on a smartphone enabling them to track positions on a desktop or smartphone and never have to transfer funds from their wallets.

- Zerion supports several web3 wallets. Since it's non-custodial, the product barely tracks positions within a wallet.

- With a few clicks, users can use Maker, Uniswap, and compound within a single dashboard.

DeFi Saver

Another one-stop asset management tool is DeFi Saver, which offers various decentralized financial protocols, including Ethereum applications.

DeFi Saver supports various protocols such as Compound and Maker, providing DeFi users with inherent and transparent management tools. In addition, the asset management application is compatible with many wallets, for instance, Coinbase, Trust, and Trezor.

In January 2019, DeFi Saver was created by the Decenter team of graphic designers, developers, and writers with a blockchain background.

DeFi Saver has excellent features that allow users to manage their DeFi portfolio with much ease.

As one of the initial DeFi products, DeFi Saver is testing a revenue model that intends to build an eco-friendly web3 model for its asset management tool.

Importance of DeFi Saver

- You can easily develop, maintain and manage a Maker vault within one location.

- DeFi Saver provides an opportunity to take part in Maker liquidations.

- You can track savings within DSR and Compound.

Bottom Line

Decentralized finance is an emerging concept within the financial market. DeFi asset management tools provide an opportunity for many global investors to join the action who never had a chance before. In addition, barriers in the traditional finance model that limited many people, such as high fees or lack of reliable financial systems, are well addressed in the DeFi ecosystem.

Section 4: What's Next?

Chapter 14 - Protecting Yourself from Scams

Yes, Scams Still Do Exist

Financial scams have been around for a while, and they can happen to anyone. Traders were scammed off exchanging goods, traditional finance has experienced scam schemes in great measure, and cryptocurrency hasn't been spared from it either. As a result, millions of crypto investors have been scammed off millions of investments in crypto coins and fiat currencies altogether.

Scammers develop crypto marks; unaware of crypto users, and scam them off on traditional finance and digital currencies. In 2018 fraud cases related to cryptocurrency amounted to the US $1.7 billion in losses. The schemes vary in size and level of technological influence daily.

In the crypto ecosystem, there are ways scams are extended to unknowing users, such as:

• Fake wallets hiding malware downloads; various attacks have come from users downloading or clicking on fake URLs posted on social media. This is primarily used to lure investors who want to trade in bitcoin; the scammers also use fake cryptocurrency surveys to distribute malware. Once this malware is planted on a device or a digital wallet, it now becomes effortless to be scammed off.

• Cryptocurrency phishing impersonators: these impersonators use social media platforms to lure investors into scams. They impersonate significant coins such as Bitcoin, Ethereum, and Litecoin to gain the users' trust; once they gain trust, they have the users key in their vital details, and they take control of the investors' wallets.

• Crypto-Flipping scams: the scammers offer a direct and instant exchange of coins for fiat currencies or vice versa. Others offer to double up the amount invested in such a short time; the deal sounds too good to be true. They never meet their end of the bargain at the end of it, and you lose coins and your currencies.

• Crypto Pyramid Schemes: they operate as a long con, and it is much harder for a trader to notice that they are being scammed; it takes a longer duration of time, more like Ponzi schemes in traditional finance. Investors who make significant investments are usually the bigger targets; the investors are asked to invite other trade partners and give them referral links. The cycle continues; a new user comes in, they are asked to recruit other users, and referral links are used, and so on. At the end of it, the amount of money brought to the establishment is a lot, and off they go with all the money.

In the technological era, most things have moved online with a click of a button. Scams using technology are the most sophisticated of all as you have almost no way to trace the scammer. Since cryptocurrency operates in a decentralized manner, it is not protected by institutions and banks; it is much harder to bring criminals to justice.

Scams come in many dimensions in the digital marketplace, which will be looked at in detail in this chapter. They cut across blockchain hacks, cybercrime, crypto loss, Ponzi schemes, fraud hidden in an Initial Coin Offering (ICO), and even manipulating the cryptocurrency market. This is accompanied by a more pressing question: how do unsuspecting crypto investors fall into fraud schemes in the first place? This is how they get to investors:

• Fast-Talking Swindlers; these scammers appeal to investors' greediness to make fast profits. It's mostly done on Telegram, the social media network used mainly through crypto traders.

• Straight-up deception: Other scammers go up straight for the lies; a specific cryptocurrency known as OneCoin runs with $3.8 billion in investments by convincing the traders that their coin was real. Others turn up as crypto genius professionals who offer help to make you wealthy, while the whole time, they were thieves.

• By exploiting friends and family: referral links, when one client gets scammed, spread that across to their family members through referral links. One time in India, Celebrities were involved in propagating a particular self-proclaimed crypto guru after he wrote a book on cryptocurrency. Not all celebrities were aware of what was going on, and so many celebrities have been duped as well, and their image portraits are being used all over social media to propagate scams and theft.

Common DeFi Scams you should be Wary of

Decentralized Finance (DeFi) is built on the Ethereum Blockchain and has unique factors compared to traditional finance. DeFi offered financial freedom to its users, freedom from the government and financial institutions that sought to control people's finances. However, as much as DeFi is trustless, that does not mean you are free from scams.

Since decentralized finance scams are on another level, they are slightly different from what you consider typical scams. For example, DeFi is online trading; the scams are online as well; here are scenarios that appear dubious on DeFi trade.

• Admin imitator; scammers come in as imitations of the actual companies or company imitators. They are on social media platforms such as Telegram, and they approach you as an admin for exchange platforms or any other services associated with DeFi. These scammers come to you presented with solutions to all the problems you would have.

• Bot Scams; in DeFi, investors use trading bots to make more profits and perfect their craft on trade. Scammers take up and make trading bots that fraudsters would later use to scam users. This is through by announcing that bugs need to be fixed, and they redirect you to another page, creating software attacks.

• Fake giveaways: crypto platforms use airdrops to raise awareness on the crypto market. Scams come in when users are contacted by fraudsters pretending to have giveaways; once you click on that information, you open ways for your wallets to be hacked. A user may also be required to pay a certain amount of money to access their giveaways, and hence you get scammed.

As long as there is a liquidity pool in the crypto market, you can always expect that there will always be scammers coming after your crypto coins. Each time there is a newly developed segment to add to the DeFi ecosystem, the hackers are always on alert to start introducing scams.

New trading opportunities such as yield farming and many trading exchanges such as Uniswap that trade in tokens have become a target for scammers. One of the worst forms of fraud in cryptocurrency is the illegal trade with which decentralized finance has come. Since it is not centralized, there is a high chance crime syndicates use it to cipher money and pay for illegal goods and services.

From now on in trade, here is a checklist to help you make the best DeFi trading choices and distinguish fake deals from the real deal:

- How does the project exist? Is it already up and running with a function-able interface, or is it a promise for tomorrow?

- Is the project innovative? If yes, then you may consider trading. If it's a no, then stay away.

- Are the developers and other investors anonymous, or are they real?

- What are their records? How have they traded, and where are their reviews?

- Get the proof of work before you invest.

- What is their current liquidity pool?

- For how long have they been in the crypto market?

Be on Guard: How to Identify Scams

Due to the decentralized nature of cryptocurrency, numerous digital currencies are released each month, with additional tokens and ICOs (Initial Coin Offerings). With this pool in the market, each new opportunity for cops in the market is a new opportunity for scammers.

DeFi is developing at a rate unprecedented with the increase in coins, and the Covid-19 pandemic has propelled the growth in DeFi. However, as an investor, if you want to stay on top of the game in trade, you need to understand that it is your sole responsibility to save yourself from scams. Below are steps to guide you to not fall into any Crypto scam.

Know the Team

Get to know the team and developers behind any coin or ICO or a trading exchange. Then, do proper research and check whether any name attached to a coin is certified and verified. An easy way to do that: is to work with coins that are developed by developers, acknowledged by big crypto developers like the developer behind Ethereum, Vitalik Buterin.

On this ground, scammers are likely to invent coins or exchange platforms by using fake names and concealing identities. To protect yourself from this scam, work on verifying the team behind every coin you invest in, check on their professional profiles on all social media platforms. In this case, they exist to go further to work out their credentials from their followers.

Pore Over the Whitepaper

The whitepaper is an essential document for the creation of any Crypto project. Whitepapers are so revealing as they outline background on the goals, strategies, and an implementation timeline of any coin created. Therefore, when deciding on the crypto trade, the first thing you should do is appropriately go through their whitepaper.

Look at everything a company is made up of, and any company that does not offer its users a whitepaper should be avoided from the very start. You may have every question as an investor should be answered by the whitepaper; if it can't do that, then walk away before making any investment.

Check the Token Sale

Any project on DeFi relies on currencies or tokens that are available for trade. To ensure that you do not get scammed, watch out for the flow of tokens over some time. Due to the open-source data and codes in the crypto market, any company that does not offer proof of work on how the coin is progressing should be avoided at all costs.

Major red flags involve secrecy in trade on ICOIs and tokens and a lack of access to the market information that investors should give a first hand.

How profitable is the project?

Many currencies are operating in the crypto ecosystem. Your success rates are determined by how achievable aims and goals are for a project or any coin. The concept a company carries must not be vague and a risk to your investment. Check on how detailed they are on investments; if the presentation looks wanting, you may already be on a target list to be scammed.

Always take caution

The idea of getting rich and quick is one you should take with utmost caution. The level of greed an investor has to make it fast in the crypto world is one aspect scammers use to defraud people. When the deal sounds too good to be true, take a step back and make a personal assessment as you make research steps.

Exit scams

These scams are the worst yet in the market; scammers lure in many investors and disappear with their investments when the money looks excellent. Due to the decentralized nature of DeFi, it is harder to track these scammers and bring them to justice. So watch out for long cons in the market.

Turning Your Back on a Scam

Scams are profitable to the scammer and a loss to the investor. Scams come in different ways in this industry; they come in the form of a person (in person), online through social media, through gadgets that are hacked, and platforms that are disbursed with malware that cause investors to lose their wealth. Here are practical ways you can take to avoid being scammed.

Question pre-sales

Typically, pre-sales are not bad as they give clients the priority to make investments before a project is launched into the market. Due to technological advancement, developers can develop a prototype of a prominent coin and sell it to unknowing investors. Research good and bad projects and what they come aligned in, and plan your investments accordingly.

Diversify

To avoid total loss in trading bitcoin and Altcoins, you may want to consider trading with various coins that are well known in the market as an investor. This enables excellent returns and eliminates the high risk of scams that come from trading one single coin.

Consider a coin's actual value.

When considering trading in a new coin, consider what that project aims to promote and achieve. Go for the fastest-growing projects and assets in the crypto market. This shows that they are doing well in the market, and whatever they are doing is profitable and brings profits. Always ask yourself if the project you are investing in is here for the long haul.

Find out more about the developers.

The anonymity of the Bitcoin founder has given the coin a high rate of survival, but that does not mean any other coin after that will achieve the same results. As an investor, research the project developers and how their identity affects how a coin will survive in the market. Also, fake founders are easily discovered when one does research, and that saves you from scams.

Study the code

You may not be a tech genius, but there is enough technical information online to help you decipher whether a code is actual or a prototype. Since the DeFi system has codes Permissionless, this could contribute to scams, but it spares you the loss on investments when you can adequately read into a scam.

Get experts views

To do better in the cryptocurrency market, you may want to follow the steps of pacesetters in this market. Listen to daily knew on what experts are saying on certain coins, how they view the trade will turn out to be, and many other aspects. This will keep you at par with trade aspects in this market. Also, it has proven that big names in the market can change the tide in how investment goes down in the recent past. An example is the recent Elon Musk involvement in cryptocurrency.

"I'm Scammed! Now What?"

As the crypto market grows daily, so are the numbers of scams because of an excellent liquidity pool and the number of more investors who are eager to invest. Unfortunately, many investors have lost their investments and are still losing; if you have been scammed trading coins, here are a few ways you can recover your investments: you can do it in two ways.

By yourself

There are some DIY (Do it yourself) steps you can take to recover your stolen cryptocurrency.

• Contact the platform that scammed you and request your investments back. Let them know that you will report them to the relevant investors if they don't return your money. This does not guarantee they will pay back the stolen money.

• If it is not returned, then report it to the proper authorities. You should, however, realize that cryptocurrency is decentralized; hence there is no central organ that deals with fraudsters.

• If these options have not worked yet, get help online by exposing the fraudsters. Make your scammed ordeal as public as you can and urge others to stop using that platform and ask for help to get your investments back still.

• Contact your digital wallet provider and have them disable your wallet if they can. Also, set them on alert that any transaction requested from your wallet, you are not the one in control of it.

Involve cryptocurrency recovery experts

If all your options seem fruitless, you may want to consider hiring crypto recovery experts at a fee. Using experts to help in recovery is the best chance one has to recover their coins due to the entire technical workforce it requires.

These experts require details to help you recover your coins; the first step would be to secure your transaction Ids. Those unique strings of letters that showcase your transactions make it very easy to recover stolen coins.

Recovering crypto from cold wallets

Cold wallets are stored on hard disks, and they can either be hacked into or physically stolen. If this happens, consider hiring an expert to help with the recovery and also trace suspects down. As an investor, you may want to consider storing your cold wallet in a vault.

Bottom line

You can stop scams before they even occur, and this requires personal responsibility. To protect your investments the best way you know how, by being alert to the fact that scams exist, always know who you are dealing with, do not click on links and emails that look suspicious. Lastly, keep personal details of the trade to yourself and do not respond to calls, emails, and messages that require remote access to your machine.

Chapter 15 - Keeping Yourself Updated

The Crypto World Moves Fast

The blockchain industry that introduced decentralized finance is one of the fastest-growing industries in finance and online trading. It is growing at a high-speed rate with new developments frequently. However, the volatility of this market is unpredictable and ever-changing, which makes it almost hard to keep up with the market as it is very overwhelming.

This chapter will look at some of the significant ways a crypto user can keep up to date with crypto news and development. The crypto industry has been under healthy volatility and unhealthy volatility (which causes extreme losses) as the market progresses. Here are some ways to keep updated about the crypto industry.

Social media platforms

A platform such as Facebook, Twitter, and Telegram, offers real-time discussions and support on cryptocurrencies that are important to investors and developers when it comes to trading cryptocurrencies. They offer every level of information, from market listings to the best tokens in the market and community support.

Websites

Some websites are dedicated to offering support to investors in crypto trading. These websites give real-time analysis and information that is circulating in the crypto market. In addition, there are project websites that offer information that is favourable to the growth of wealth while trading.

News outlets

As there has always been business news analyzing forex trading and the stock market, cryptocurrency has been added to the list. In addition, journalist outlets such as blogs, cable news, and television news cover crypto daily. Thus, day Trading is made efficient by on-time news that influences trade.

Analyzing Data Tools

The use of some of the best data analytical tools in the crypto market will put you on top of the carts in making profits. Major investors have learned the tools required to interpret charts and graphs that contain vital crypto trading information. When you know this field, it becomes easier to keep up with crypto trades.

Experts Advice

Some people have found it easy to trade in this market; these crypto geniuses offer trade advice on many social media outlets such as blogs, TV interviews, YouTube channels, and podcasts. As a trader, you may consider listening to the most credible experts to better your trading journey.

First-Hand Experience

Even with all the research one can do, nothing beats having some experience trading cryptocurrency. Through participation, one can learn the trade tools, which makes it possible to note developing trends and keep up with them as they come.

Have an Education

Like any other form of trade and business investments in traditional finance taught and learned, the same can apply to cryptocurrency. Blockchain has turned around the world of finance, and they are time-consuming; since the future of finance and trade is in cryptocurrency; you may want to consider getting an education to survive the market.

Understanding Market Volatility

More often than not, extreme volatility has negative impacts on crypto trading, while healthy volatility is favourable and keeps the market at a reasonable margin of losses. To be up on your game in trading, you need to understand how the constant volatility affects the market and its trading power. So please get to know the coin you are investing in and its volatility in the market.

Understand What the Market Entails

Decentralized finance is the future of finance, and with it comes developmental issues daily. Keep yourself up to date with every aspect that makes up DeFi, and with it, each trading aspect plays a huge role in how trade occurs every day. Learn DeFi Lingo so that you have a quick understanding of what is happening whenever it's mentioned anywhere.

Even in its early days of development, cryptocurrency can grow into the best financial system the world has experienced so far. It has an offer of financial freedom, has many innovation aspects, and has made quite an offer that has it sticking out in the market. Of course, nothing is a hundred percent in confirmation of how the future will unfold, but cryptocurrency is promising.

Analytical Tools and Project Websites

Cryptocurrency is a financial trading system that operates 24/7, and it is worldwide. Volatility is how this market operates, which means one has to be at the top of their game to stay relevant in the crypto industry. Tools are of great use; when it comes to making profits and securing your investments. Here are some of the tools and project websites to help you stay relevant.

Before you get to using these tools and following any bit of advice on these websites, note that they will not replace your judgment and capacity to make decisions. With that in mind, the best thing would be to select the best tools and websites available; which are:

1. Cryptocompare

It is one of the best tools for comprehensive analysis, and it deals with technical analysis. It offers the best services for in-depth information on many fundamental analysis aspects in the market. At Cryptocompare, you will find many information on hundreds of coins, their prices, charts, and technical data. In addition, they provide mining calculators, educational guides and trading strategies, and many solutions for problems in the market.

2. Coin360

This platform has a straightforward interface of graphical designs that allows a person to make a visual interpretation of data in charts and graphs.

Their visual maps are presented in blocks, and these blocks are marked with colours that enable interpretation.

3. Blockfolio

This is one of the essential analytical tools in the market; with so many coins floating in the market, it offers well-analyzed data that makes trading very easy. Blockfolio has more than 5000 cryptocurrencies in its listing, with occasional additional and one can track them effortlessly on their websites. In addition, it offers trading volume on more than 300 exchanges, and they have aggregators used to track prices.

4. eToro

EToro offers multi-purpose services for crypto traders, and it is both a trading platform and it also offers analytical tools for the trade. In addition, it offers the investor a watch list to keep trading crypto, analyzed charts, and social trading features where one learns from other people in the crypto ecosystem.

5. Delta Crypto Portfolio App

It allows an investor an opportunity to track more than 5000 cryptocurrencies and set an alert to help track their prices and decide whether to trade or not. In addition, it has unique features that help a client view trading history and analyze it still. Lastly, it can sync up different devices that you own to get trading information from anywhere, and it analyses different trading portfolios.

6. TradingView

It is one of the best trading websites that offer technical analysis and a social network for entrepreneurs. It offers different trade frames of information in charts that have analyzed data for suitable trading. Its offer comes in three different categories that are PRO, PRO+, and Premium.

7. CoinMarket Cap

It's a free online marketing platform with price volatility and market price for coins existing in the crypto market. The information they offer is all around as it offers historical data analysis for prices and market capitalization over the last 24 hours.

If you understand how to use these tools and decipher the information provided, trading will be much easier. It is your sole responsibility to decide what material you will use for trade.

Using Social Media as News Source

Technology ushered the digital era, and many things have become globalized. Social media has been used to grow and propagate the cryptocurrency era in recent years. In the last years, the value of the cryptocurrency has skyrocketed, and so has its popularity among netizens. There are many differences between digital finance and traditional finance, and social media has played a significant role in it.

Crypto and Social media

In the last two decades, social media has changed how we live our everyday lives to the extent that it's been used to gauge the importance of what is happening in society. To some extent, it has been believed that if something, a trend, or products or services aren't trending on social media, then they don't exist.

Social media outlets promote cryptocurrencies, such as Twitter, Facebook, YouTube, blogs, and Telegram. In 2021 Facebook started to consider cryptocurrency a new way to invest; they are formulating their coin.

When it comes to social media, anything is possible as it carries both sides of the coin. However, some pros and cons are associated with using the media to promote cryptocurrency. As much as it's used to serve the positive nature of the crypto market, Social Media can also use it to trash the market. One negative word concerning a coin and it flops in minutes.

Crypto changing the digital market

With peer-to-peer systems of digital finance, it's much harder to collect consumer information due to the privacy that comes with the blockchain network. Due to this, producers find it hard to know the real-time market value of some products associated with cryptocurrencies.

Crypto transactions allow users to buy goods and services in absolute anonymity; this leaves small digital prints stiff for start-up companies to sustain a new product in the market. Marketers have faced severe hiccups, and this is bound to continue even in the latter days, so cryptocurrency is changing social media entrepreneurship.

Digital marketing

When trading in bitcoin or Altcoins, it has a ripple effect. First, one takes their fiat currency or assets and uses them to buy their coins. After that, one trades in these coins and makes a profit; there is a need to spend it on online marketing. Due to this trading system, many business owners have moved to the social media platform and have started accepting crypto as a payment method.

As crypto picks up soon, business owners may be forced to join the crypto market to secure buyers that operate in the new financial system. However, the role of cryptocurrency on digital marketing and social media platforms is still foggy without a much-needed direction on trade.

Cryptocurrency is going through normal processes that other financial systems went through before they were fully established. When fiat currency came about, the world never really gave up barter trade, and right now, it won't be any different. The best-case scenario would be cryptocurrency working hand in hand with the other forms of finance, and social media has been a great help to achieve that and faster.

Having a Network will help a lot.

As the infamous ancient saying goes, your network is your net worth; it isn't any different in the crypto market. Investors, who are serious about trading cryptocurrency, need a strong network of support and trade to get by in the new financial era. Investors and developers can achieve this support through Discord and Telegram in the best of ways.

Crypto in Discord

Discord is a voice app created for gamers and has now been taken over by crypto users. It has been proved to be more secure because of its free voice aspect and name recognition. In Discord, the crypto operates in Discord Webhook or Discord bot. For the bot to work, the platform receives a configuration file with cryptocurrencies Ids and how they work in the crypto market.

Developers released Discord in 2015 with the game's sole purpose, but political and entertainment sectors later picked it to include lifestyle and now cryptocurrency. Its interface offers real-time communication for investors, and above that, it has the following aspects:

• Relevant for target audiences; developers prefer Discord when targeting specific users in crypto for blockchain communications.

• There is direct feedback; both experts (developers) and investors can communicate on this platform and get direct feedback on investments and any questions.

• Cultivate a Trusted environment; for developers, this is a unique platform to build clientele, and it's very secure, tested, and approved.

Crypto Telegram

At the dawn and progression of the Global Pandemic in 2020, the crypto community set up camp on Telegram, and ever since, it has been used to gather detailed market information on cryptocurrency. In addition, Telegram offered its investors and developers anonymity and encrypted charts.

Currently, Telegram has grown to have channel lists and discussion groups that offer community support to the crypto ecosystem. Some of the best telegram channel lists include; Binance announcement, CoinGape, today we push, and Margin whales. All these chandelles are dedicated to offering the best daily news, discussions, analysis, and technical support.

More channels and groups are operating on Telegram; it has become more prevalent in the crypto community because it has the best security and customer service features. Some of the prominent groups on Telegram include:

- ICO speaks news has more than 450,000 subscribers and provides the best news on ICO DeFi reviews and Blockchain news, among other news on buying and selling cryptocurrency.

- DeFi Million has more than 400,000 subscribers and over 1 million users in DeFi, and it's one of the first telegram channels with their token DEMI, and it offers announcements and a platform for start-ups.

- IEO pools have the latest news on marketing and listings of crypto assets.

- BTC champ is a Telegram platform that offers sales and purchases of

cryptocurrency.

Telegram offers you private or public groups, and it's up to you to choose what you want. For public groups, you can join by simply clicking on the join button, while for the private groups; you have to request to be added as a member.

Doing Your Homework

Cryptocurrency can be complicated for first-time investors; if you have been in the crypto market long enough, you know that research is the only way to the top and that advice from others can prove futile. When you follow other people's opinions on trade, you are always left with unanswered questions.

Doing your research comes in handy as you will understand the crypto market better; the more tools you gather, the better your trade. Here are some research methodologies that can aid you in maximizing the crypto world.

• Exploring social media platforms such as Telegram, Twitter, Facebook and YouTube will yield good results. The masses in the crypto trade have thrived because of the social media exposure cryptocurrencies have received. These platforms are social-community support systems that offer insights at a click of a button.

• Analyzing upcoming events brings out the global aspects of the crypto market. If events are coming up that means growth of the crypto market; they would be an excellent place to start. Also, some events mean doom for the coins, which would mean it's a perfect time not to invest.

• Research the fundamental aspects of Bitcoin and Altcoins. As an investor, you want to know the actual market value of the crypto coins you want to invest in research their Smart Contracts, tokens, and liquidity pools.

• Acquaint yourself with trending topics; one of the best ways to stay on top of the chain is to look at the current affairs in the crypto market. Have the upper hand advantage on what is coming into the market.

• Check on the technical data; your research should include a proper understanding of technicalities in the crypto coins. Check on the market capitalization of the new coins in the market and those that have existed before. Seek to understand how the coin exists, and it's circulating supply, token distribution, and emission rates.

• Understand the market and community; understand trading platforms and exchanges for the investments you are already making. Research the best places to trade your coins and the community that backs the coin. On that line, make sure to research places you can buy goods and services using cryptocurrency.

• Lastly, learn about cryptocurrency fraud and scams. Like any other market, you must understand there are criminals out here to squander your investments. Do the research it takes to understand the pros and cons of investing in cryptocurrencies.

For better returns as you trade, it is important as an investor or a developer to take full advantage of social media. In the current times, social media has become a great support for publicity and product promotion. On the other hand, research is important as it helps you to filter through the truth and lies easily.

CONCLUSION

Technology has brought with it a new financial era that is Cryptocurrency. In the past, people relied on traditional needs to; live a good life, make purchases, and acquire goods and services. Every aspect of our lives, political, social, and economic, has been lived through Fiat currencies. It has its pros and cons; one thing, though, has stood out and brought about decentralized finance.

Cryptocurrency is and has been offering financial security above all. It offers freedom from institutions and governments that seek to control finance and limit investments. For the very first time, we have a global market that works to the advantage of developed, developing, and third world countries under the umbrella of Cryptocurrency.

Crypto has become a trend for a while now, and this book has been written to enable all investors who want to begin to trade in the crypto market to be aware of the steps to take. The future of trade and financial freedom lies in Cryptocurrency; this could be the high time you begin trading before the market gets overly competitive.

Before you begin trading, there are a few things you may want to understand, and they are encompassed in this book. First, there are numerous Altcoins and other notable fields in trade; the difference they come with should be duly noted and researched on before you put up your money for investments.

In this book, Decentralized Finance (DeFi) has been thoroughly worked at to help you as an investor to make solid decisions. It covers DeFi from its start to how it's progressing to date and its ups and downs. Better yet, the DeFi lingual has now been made familiar. All you have to do is get into trading, and all will make sense to you.

Worth noting is that DeFi has enabled trade; that is, purchasing and selling, and with DeFi, an investor can yield profits in trade. This is made possible by the blockchain built on ethereum that supports DeFi. The DeFi ecosystem comprises Smart Contracts, stablecoins, ledgers, marketplaces and exchanges alongside asset management and insurance platforms.

Would you want to start using Bitcoin or Altcoins as a currency to purchase and pay for goods and services? That has been made possible because of stablecoins that combine crypto coins and fiat currencies such as the US Dollar or the Sterling UK Pound. Stable coins are what will be used to replace traditional financial currencies in the global market.

Before you start to trade, understand the Crypto market and how it operates to see if you would like to invest or not. Then, weigh in your options, the amount of money you want to invest, the timeframe you expect your profits. It is your personal choice whether to invest or not.

As an investor, understand the crypto-financial systems just like you understood currencies in traditional finance. Understanding fiat-to-crypto exchanges, crypto wallets, and their banks, in addition, understand crypto-to-crypto- exchanges. These four elements play a crucial role in crypto transactions for individuals and institutions that deal in crypto.

In traditional finance, there was theft and scams, and that hasn't changed in online marketplaces. The only difference is most of the time, the theft and scamming take place on online platforms. This book discusses users' security concerns in the modern era of crypto finance and how to navigate them.

Research is fundamental to this market, and there is no better way to put how crucial personal research is. There are elements of the Crypto ecosystem that you need to understand. Personally, this information will spare you losses and wrong interpretation of what is happening daily on the global market.

The crypto market is not what it was a decade ago, more complexities have come in, and mining coins has become more complex, time-consuming, and takes up most of your resources. Since this is a decentralized unit, all the benefits of a centralized banking system no longer exist. As an investor and a developer, get decentralized insurance to secure your investments from the volatile nature of Cryptocurrency.

The excellent part about trading crypto is the ability to shop and pay with earned crypto profits. Many institutions and private/public entities have started accepting crypto as a means of payment in recent times. Some governments are getting to a point they want to legalize crypto as a payment method. In the past, there haven't been legal or illegal grounds to measure crypto on, and that debate looks like it's coming to an end.

Many aspects are being added to the DeFi ecosystem to allow all financial systems to operate in the market. This is like taking out loans, participating in lotteries, and offering human services to a computerized environment like being a broker or an asset guardian to assets put on the crypto market like gold and silver.

To maximize your investments, you need to keep yourself updated on the global crypto market and protect yourself from scams and hacks. Of course, this is easier said than done, which is why there are community support systems in almost all the social media platforms to help with that.

The cryptocurrency market is still a big question that needs to be answered as the actual world figures out the future of Cryptocurrency. Many questions are ranging in regards to how safe and how far will this market go? However, the answer is in our present, and as of now, the crypto market thrives, and more people are investing in it.

Please, do not miss out on this opportunity that technology has offered us. As a beginner, many things are uncertain, but few things are certain; that the future of finance is in Cryptocurrency, and the investment is worth every coin. Decentralized finance has stabilized the market through stable coins and filled so many missing links earlier experienced at the start of the crypto market.

More coins are being formulated, more investors coming into the market, the blockchain technology is getting smarter and the global market has accepted cryptocurrency. I wonder what would stop the future of Crypto trade.